antique & collectible
Buttons
IDENTIFICATION & VALUES
VOLUME II

DEBRA J. WISNIEWSKI

COLLECTOR BOOKS

A Division of Schroeder Publishing Co., Inc.

The current values in this book should be used only as a guide. They are not intended to set prices, which vary from one section of the country to another. Auction prices as well as dealer prices vary greatly and are affected by condition as well as demand. Neither the author nor the publisher assumes responsibility for any losses that might be incurred as a result of consulting this guide.

Cover design by Beth Summers
Book design by Terri Hunter
Photography by Charles R. Lynch

Searching For A Publisher?

We are always looking for people knowledgeable within their fields. If you feel that there is a real need for a book on your collectible subject and have a large comprehensive collection, contact Collector Books.

COLLECTOR BOOKS
P.O. Box 3009
Paducah, Kentucky 42002-3009

www.collectorbooks.com

Copyright © 2002 Debra J. Wisniewski

Contents

Dedication

This book is dedicated to all who have been bitten by the button bug.

About the Author

Debra Wisniewski has been involved in her family's estate auctioneering business since 1970. She has served as president and as secretary of the West Michigan Buttoneers and is a member of the National Button Society. She continues to spread the joy of button collecting at schools, historical societies, and civic groups.

Acknowledgments

I would like to express my appreciation to all my fellow button collectors, and button book authors, both past and present. You have shared your research and knowledge with all of us, through articles in state and national bulletins, *Just Buttons* magazines, and in book form. To the studio buttons artist's thank you, for graciously answering all my questions. Thanks, goes to Bud and Connie Wiser for supplying me with many of the mounting cards you will see through out this book. To Dr. Roger Revell who helped with questions and prices on the boxed sets. To Nancy and Skip DuBois who are such close friends, thank you, for all your moral support.

A very special thank you to my husband Tim, and our two oldest children Tyler and Ashley. To our youngest child, Dylan, manuscripts are not for scribbling in or dripping your bottle on. Buttons do not go in your mouth, down the heat vents, or in the wastebasket when mommy is not looking. To my mom and dad, Jane and Gordon Barlow, thank you for all the hours you watched Dylan for me. Without my family and friends, I would not have been able to do this again.

A special thanks to Lisa Stroup. Not only has she been my editor, but she has been my friend and has helped me through the whole process of producing a beautiful book. Thank you also to the dedicated staff at Collector Books for all their hard work and perseverance. Without these people, this book would never have been realized.

Introduction

In this second book of *Antique & Collectible Buttons*, I have used the same format as book one. You will see the same types of buttons as the first book, but hopefully no exact duplicates. Differences found between the two books are a larger studio button section, more paperweights and a few pages on newly manufactured buttons. I am hoping the additional text will be welcome and after reading it, you will go away feeling you have learned a little more about the hobby so many of us enjoy.

DJW

National Button Society official sizes
Large: $1\frac{1}{4}$" and over
Medium: $\frac{3}{4}$" to $1\frac{1}{4}$"
Small: $\frac{3}{8}$" to $\frac{3}{4}$"
Diminutive: Up to $\frac{3}{8}$"

Left: Advertising Trade Card
Bottom: February 14, 1896 Waterbury Button Company invoice. There were 23 gross of buttons ordered for a total price of $89.62.

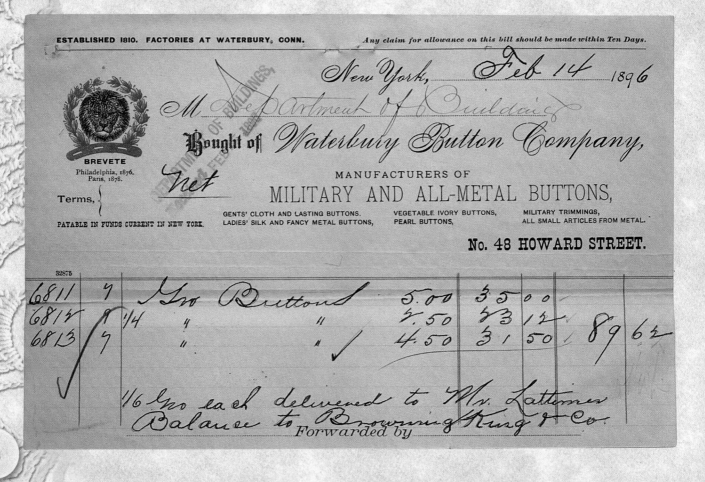

AMERICAN BUTTON COMPANY
MANUFACTURES

MILITARY BUTTONS

LADIES FANCY METAL BUTTONS

YOUTHS GILT BUTTONS

ALL-METAL BUTTONS

BELT BUCKLES AND CLASPS

METAL BADGES OF ALL KINDS

MILITARY TRIMMINGS

ALL NOVELTIES FROM SHEET METAL

70 MORRIS AVE.

Terms *Net Cash 30 days*

Newark, N.J., April 5, 1904

Sold to The Public Service Co. of N. J. 776 Broad St, City.

Package	No.	Gross							
	1046	1	Plain Cnt	Nickel Spec.		3 00	✓	3 00	
	1047	6	--	Vest	--	--	1 50	✓	9 00
#604	470	21	Cmd Scroll Cnt	Gilt	--	3 00	✓	63 00
	471	18	-- -- Vest	--	--	1 50	✓	27 00
	450	12	Mtr -- Cnt	Nickel	--	3 00	✓	36 00
	451	21	-- -- Vest	--		1 50	✓	31 50 / 169 50

Shipped to North Jersey St. Ry.,

21 Hudson Place, Hoboken, N.J.

Order # 371

En Adams Ex.

F. O. B. DESTINATION.

CHECKED H.M.

VOUCHERED

APR 1904

538

1904 American Button Company Invoice
A total of $169.50 for 79 gross of buttons that included an assortment of nickel and gilt buttons in two different sizes.
They were sold to "The Public Service Center of New Jersey" and delivered to the "Street Railway Department."

Left: This display rack shows a variety of frames and deluxe bottom mounting boards available from Connie and Bud Weiser. They are regular attendees at national and many state shows. In addition to button collecting supplies, they also carry a wide range of antique buttons for purchase.

Below: On special request, Bud will make up boards to get just the right color combination for displaying your buttons.

The Millennium is here!

Black carved Bakelite, metal escutcheon
and green glass cabochon center. Large,
$20.00 – 30.00.

Apple juice colored Bakelite
with a carved leaf on each
side and sequin embellishment.
Large, $10.00 – 15.00.

"V" for Victory, three-color
Bakelite. Medium, $30.00.

Brown Bakelite with metal escutcheon
and pink cabochon in center. Large,
$20.00 – 25.00.

Bakelite "Cookie" buttons. Small, $3.00. Medium, $5.00 – 7.00. Large, $8.00 – 10.00.

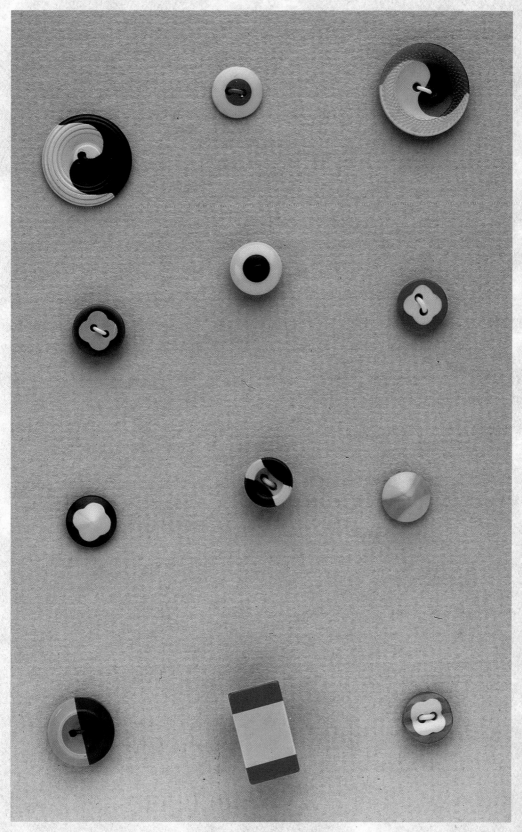

Bakelite "Cookie" buttons. Small, $3.00 – 5.00. Medium, $6.00.

*Charles Dana Gibson and Howard Chandler Christy were popular illustrators during the late Victorian and early Edwardian periods. I have seen this button titled both Gibson Girl and Christy Girl. I feel either title is appropriate since both artists portrayed women with upswept hair and elongated facial and neck features. Black Bakelite with metal escutcheon.
Large, $25.00 – 35.00.*

*Black Bakelite with decorative metal border and white metal rat.
$80.00 – 95.00.*

*Concave chocolate brown Bakelite with rooster head escutcheon.
Large, $65.00 – 80.00.*

*Dark brown carved Bakelite with metal thistle escutcheon.
Large, $35.00 – 45.00.*

Black Bakelite with anchor.
Medium, $15.00 – 18.00.

Green Bakelite, carved oval.
Medium, $10.00 – 12.00.

Reverse carved, Bakelite with dyed and painted backs.
Medium, left, $18.00; right, $12.00.

Ten-hole, medium, $10.00. Star, small, $5.00. Odd shape, small, $5.00. Gears, large, $8.00.

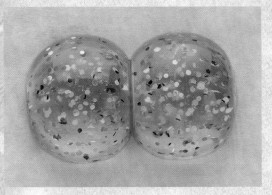

Apple juice colored Bakelite with sparkles.
Large, $12.00 – 16.00.

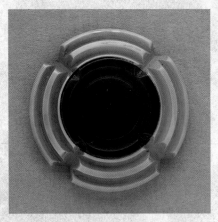

Carved butterscotch Bakelite
with green center.
Medium, $8.00 – 12.00.

Lady golfer in concave
brown Bakelite.
Medium, $18.00 – 22.00.

Green barbell-shaped Bakelite
with metal. Medium, $8.00.

Bakelite hearts.
Medium, $8.00. Cupid, $15.00 – 18.00. Arrow, $8.00 – 10.00.

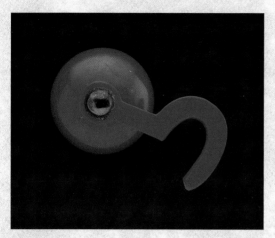

Red Bakelite with celluloid or plastic hook.
Large, $12.00 – 15.00.

Bakelite, tri-color star. Medium,
$8.00 – 10.00.

Carved green Bakelite.
Large, $15.00 – 18.00.

Butterscotch and black laminated Bakelite.
Large, $12.00 – 15.00.

Black Glass

Black glass buttons became popular during the reign of Queen Victoria. Victoria was born in Kensington Palace on May 24, 1819, the only child of Edward, Duke of Kent, and Princess Victoria, daughter of the Duke of Saxe-Coburg. Victoria's father died of pneumonia when she was only eight months old. She led a very sheltered life in her early years. Several of her uncles, cousins, and a grandfather died because of illness or old age when she was young. Her mother, who was very controlling, feared that the remaining family members in line for the throne might do great harm to her. Victoria slept in the same room as her mother until she became queen at the age of 18 and demanded her own room.

Victoria first met her cousin Albert when she was 16 years old, and nothing became of it then but friendship. When she again saw Albert, she fell in love. Victoria was very drawn to his good looks and wrote about him in her diary. Although he was a duke, Albert was penniless, and it was to his and his family's advantage that he marry Victoria. Victoria and Albert married on February 10, 1840 and had nine children together. She was a very independent woman at first, and they had a very happy marriage. Victoria came to depend on Albert's advice and opinion on all court matters, as her love for him grew.

On December 14, 1861, her beloved Albert died of typhoid fever. After his death, Victoria kept herself in seclusion at Osborne or Balmoral. For a long period, she neglected her responsibilities as queen, but in her later years she was more attentive to her role. In respect for the Queen's mourning of Albert, jet became even more popular. Black glass quickly replaced jet, and so began the abundance of this material found in every old button box and collection. Queen Victoria continued to wear black until her death in 1901.

"Ariel". A difficult button to find in this size and material, even with the chips at 12 and 3 o'clock. Large, $50.00, more if in excellent condition.

Kate Greenaway design called Spring, with silver luster. Medium, $35.00.

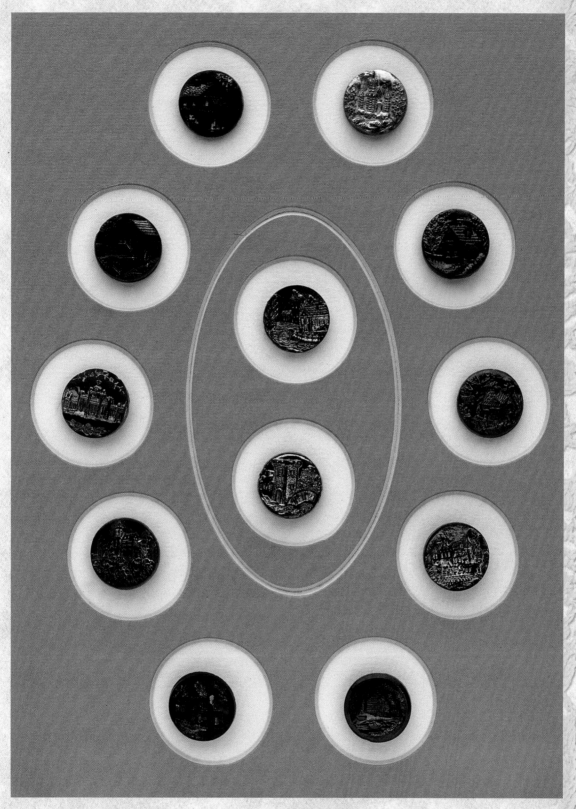

Architectural scenes, assorted luster and paint finishes. All but one are NBS small.
$7.00 – 12.00.

Shell, silver luster.
Medium, $10.00 – 15.00.

Black glass
pictorials.
Small,
$8.00 – 12.00.

Wheat, 1¼". Large, $20.00 – 25.00.

Fabulous animals with assorted luster and paint finishes. Small, $6.00 – 8.00.

Pictorial objects, small, assorted lusters.
Checkerboard, $10.00. Arrow, $4.00. Dice, $8.00. Shell, $7.00. Coin type, $15.00 – 18.00. Basket, $8.00.

Flies and beetles. Small, $8.00 – 12.00.

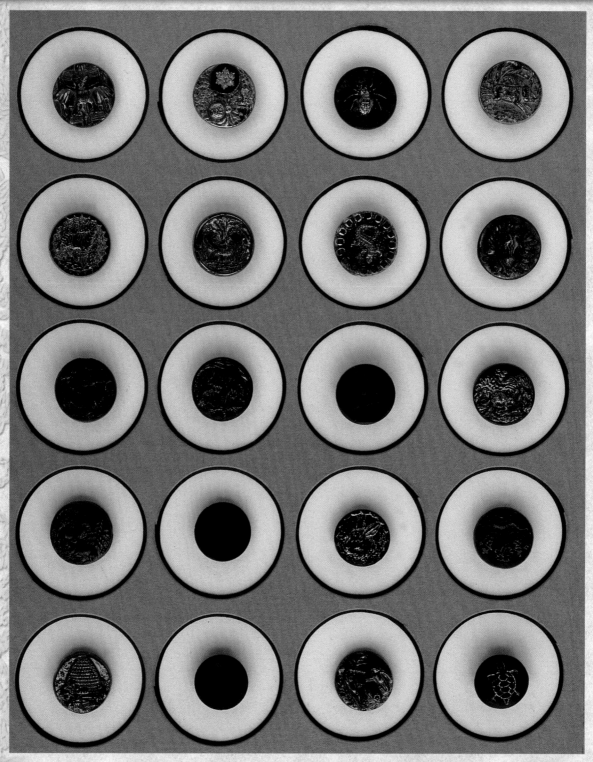

Black glass, small, plain and assorted lusters.

Bat, $12.00 – 15.00.
Zebra, $12.00 – 16.00.
Lion, $10.00 – 12.00.
Deer, $7.00 – 9.00.
Bee hive, $7.00 – 10.00.

Spider and fly, $7.00 – 9.00.
Snake, $15.00 – 18.00.
Jumbo the Elephant, $10.00 – 12.00
Jumping deer, $5.00 – 7.00.
Fish, $6.00 – 8.00.

Spider, $8.00 – 10.00.
Salamander, $5.00 – 7.00.
Platypus, $18.00 – 20.00.
Rabbit, $8.00 – 10.00.
Frogs and snail, $10.00 – 12.00.

Pig, $8.00 – 10.00.
Frog, $12.00 – 15.00.
Rat, $10.00 – 12.00.
Rabbit, $7.00 – 9.00.
Turtle, $7.00 – 10.00.

*Oriental scene, two women on a boat and
a man with raised arms, on shore, 1⁹/₁₆".
Large, $75.00 – 90.00.*

*Shepherdess, 1¹/₁₆".
Medium, $25.00 – 30.00.*

*Architectural scenes, assorted lusters, ¹⁵/₁₆" to 1¹/₁₆", medium.
Left to right: $35.00, $30.00, $35.00, $20.00, $35.00.*

*Black glass, small.
Kate Greenaway, $20.00. Cherub, $20.00. Mythological Diana, $8.00. Oriental, $10.00.*

Castle scene, 1¹⁄₁₆".
Medium, $18.00 – 22.00.

Athena, Bellerophon, and Pegasus,
dull black glass insert set in a shiny
black glass rim. Large, $75.00 – 90.00.

Ivy on trellis by brick wall, 1¼".
Medium, $20.00 – 30.00.

Black glass with silver luster, mediums.
St. Hubert's Hounds, $15.00. Horse head, $20.00.

Fans, one with silver luster and one with gold
luster. NBS mediums, $15.00 – 20.00 each.

Buckle buttons. Medium, $15.00 – 18.00 each.

Dogs. Small, $8.00 – 10.00 each.

*Architectural scenes with assorted lusters and paint finishes.
Small, $6.00 – 8.00 each.*

*Croquet, back-marked with the
British Registry mark.
Medium, $15.00 – 20.00.*

Black glass with fired-on enamel paint, small and medium.
Florals and leaves, $5.00 – 8.00. Bird, blue and white enamel surrounded by gold luster, $10.00.
Archer, multicolored enamels, $8.00. Swan, $15.00. Fly, multicolored enamel, $12.00.

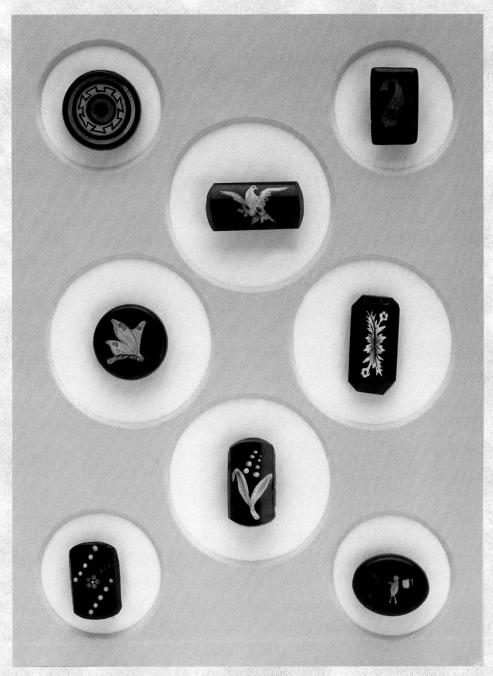

Black glass with fired-on enamel paint, small and medium.
Dove, $12.00. Corn, $8.00. Butterfly, $15.00. All others, $5.00 – 7.00 each.

Black glass, plain and assorted lusters, small.
Crane, $5.00. Bird on birdhouse, $8.00 – 10.00. Bird by flowers, $6.00. Swan, $12.00 – 15.00.

Bird on trellis, vines, just over 1¼".
Large, $30.00 – 35.00.

Soldier's head.
Medium, $15.00 – 20.00.

Guy in rowboat under tree, ¹⁵/₁₆".
Medium, $10.00 – 15.00.

Butterfly, 1⅛".
Medium, $20.00 – 25.00.

Owls, small and medium.
Top row, left to right:
Lifelike glass eyes, $25.00 – 35.00.
Sitting on crescent and stars, $10.00 – 12.00.
Bottom row, left to right:
Head, $12.00 – 15.00.
Head cemented on oblong black glass, $15.00.

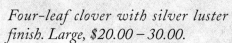

Four-leaf clover with silver luster
finish. Large, $20.00 – 30.00.

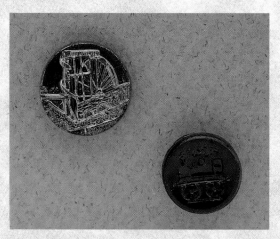

Top: Lady Isabella is a water wheel that was built in
1854. It stands 72½ feet high and claims to be Europe's
largest water wheel. Use of the wheel for mining was
discontinued in 1929. In 1965, it was purchased and
restored by the government and continues to be a great
tourist attraction, ¾", $8.00.
Bottom: Train, ⅝", $8.00.

Lady's head. Medium, $12.00.

What is it?
Civil War-style shield, society or school
emblem or musical instrument called a lyre?
I am still researching, since I find this a very
interesting old black glass button. $8.00.

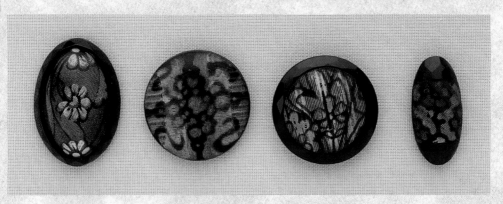

Black glass with paint finish imitating fabric.
Medium and large, $8.00 – 15.00 each.

Buckles. Small, $8.00 – 10.00 each.

Vintage black glass buttons. All are medium except for bottom left and right.

$5.00	$6.00	$4.00	$4.00
$4.00	$6.00	$4.00	$3.00
$8.00	$6.00	$5.00	$6.00

Old black glass, small and medium.
Stein, $15.00. Castle, $8.00. Lion's Head, $10.00. Fan, $8.00.
Couple, $12.00. Square w/paisley, $6.00. Lizard, $7.00. All others, $3.00 – 5.00 each.

Old black glass squares, medium and large, plain black glass and assorted lusters. Various shanks consisting of loop shank, loop shank and plate, and four-way box shank with thread grooves. I have been working on this card for several years, and it is a lot harder to find these in different patterns than one might think. $10.00 – 15.00 each.

Small openwork black glass with two and three hole sew-thrus, others with metal shanks. Though inexpensive, these buttons can take a while to collect. Pear, $8.00 – 10.00. Others, $4.00 – 6.00 each.

Old black glass, small.
Left row: Tile, $12.00 – 15.00. Brass escutcheon, $10.00 – 15.00. Men's vest
button, $8.00 – $10.00.
Center row: Watch crystal, $35.00. (Author's note: More appropriate to glass category.)
Pink foil butterfly paperweight, $30.00 – 35.00.
Right row: Tinque, $85.00 – 100.00. Center rose and tiny flowers are inlaid,
the green leaves and blue are painted on, $8.00.
Men's vest button, $8.00 – 10.00.

Black glass with glass overlay, silver luster, sterling silver paint, enamel paints, reverse painted glass set in glass, and plain black glass. Large.

Row 1: $12.00	Row 2: $15.00	Row 3: $22.00
$12.00	$12.00	$15.00
$10.00	$18.00	$8.00
	$15.00	

Black glass plant life, small.
Wheat, $6.00. Wheat, $5.00. Rose, $7.00. William Tell's apple, $8.00 – 10.00.
Insect on persimmon, $6.00.

Small black glass with four-metal box shank.
Left to right: Silver foil paperweight. Goldstone and glass overlay roses.
Rose paperweight. Colored foil and glass overlay stripes.
Glass overlay rose, twisted ribbon and goldstone.
$6.00 – 8.00 each.

Baby in the water with upheld arms, a stork looks on. What is the story behind this fabulous small button? $20.00.

Egyptian woman's head, 1⅛".
Medium, $30.00.

Recently imported black glass from the Czech Republic. Luster finishes on these newer buttons are bolder and brighter. The metal loop shank and plate found on some can confuse new collectors because it is so similar to the shank used on old buttons. $5.00 – 8.00 each.

Thistle, just under 1¼".
Medium, $18.00 – 22.00.

Precision inlays, $15.00 and $10.00.

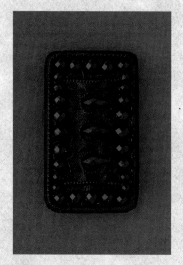

Buckle design, unique oblong shape,
¹¹⁄₁₆" x 1⅛". Medium, $15.00 – 18.00.

Two small buttons with a brown paint finish, imitating wood,
$6.00 each.

Camel, celluloid bubble-top.
Medium, $10.00 – 15.00.

Painted metal, horse-racing cart,
set in celluloid. Medium, $10.00.

Metal, fabulous creature
mounted on celluloid.
Large, $10.00 – 15.00.

Pierced celluloid,
$1^5/_{16}$", $10.00.

Fabulous molded and
painted peacock on a
celluloid disc, set in a
scallop-edged celluloid
frame, $2^5/_{16}$",
$35.00 – 50.00.

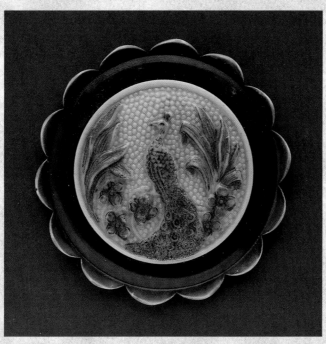

Thick one-piece celluloid, picturing Oriental men, symbols, and bamboo. Just under 2",
$20.00 – 30.00.

Celluloid top with black lacquered metal back,
2⅛", $15.00 – 20.00.

Two-piece hollow celluloid with
fabric flowers inside.
Medium, $8.00.

Black celluloid sew-thru, with an
impressed flower basket, silver paint
in the background.
Large, $10.00.

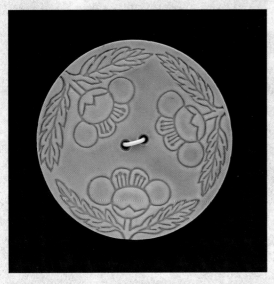

Large sew-thru celluloid disc with impressed floral pattern, $12.00 – 15.00.

This very large celluloid button has 46 rhinestones surrounded by silver paint and a metal loop shank, 1¹⁵/₁₆", $12.00 – 15.00.

Large black celluloid with paint-filled lines of a lighthouse scene, $18.00 – 25.00.

Huge celluloid button with wavy lines and a floral pattern, 3½" x 1½", single celluloid shank, $15.00 – 20.00.

Assorted celluloid buttons, including celluloid backgrounds and perforates.
Embellishments include pearls, cut steels, and paste.
Top row: $15.00, $22.00, $15.00.
Center row: $38.00, $20.00.
Bottom row: $18.00, $20.00, $15.00.

One-piece Thirties, a term collectors have given this specific type of pictorial celluloid button. They have cemented-on celluloid shanks or are sew-thrus. Large.
Ship, $30.00. Hunting dogs, $15.00. Horse racing, $20.00. Football players, $15.00 each.
Airplanes, $18.00 each. Football, $10.00. Anchor, $12.00.

Extruded celluloid buttons, medium to large, $8.00 – 12.00 each.

A separate celluloid cicada, held in place by three brass pins on a 2" disc, wire loop shank. $40.00.

Two-piece hollow celluloid with paint-filled lines, attached hump shank. Large, $25.00 – 35.00.

Art Deco design on a large one-piece celluloid. with metal loop shank inserted into celluloid base, $7.00 – 10.00.

Square celluloid one-piece with hump shank, $10.00 – 15.00.

These buttons are first coated with paint, then
the high spots are "buffed" to remove the paint
and expose the design in white.
Duck, $8.00. Couple, $8.00. Vogue, $10.00.

1⁹⁄₁₆" one-piece celluloid picturing palm trees,
pyramids, and bird, with attached
celluloid shank, $20.00 – 30.00.

Cherries, celluloid hump shank.
Medium, $10.00 – 15.00.

Hollow, two-piece floral celluloid.
Large, $10.00 – 15.00.

Ceramic

Satsuma buttons are one of the most sought-after types of ceramic buttons among collectors. Quite a selection is available, and prices vary greatly depending on subject matter, age, and condition. You can tell the older ones by their lower, rounded shank and long, threaded grooves. Curved thread grooves are another good sign that the button is older. Modern Satsuma buttons have a high, sharp-edged shank and generally no thread grooves, but there are exceptions. Sizes range from small to medium.

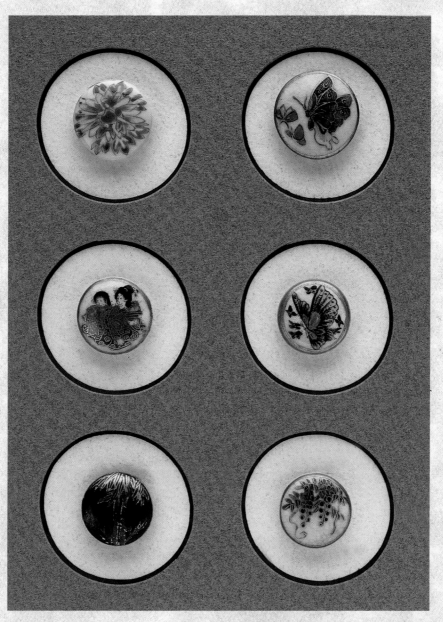

Old, floral, gold rim worn, $15.00.
Old, women, gold dots in background, $30.00.
Modern, cobalt blue, 1940s, $15.00.

Modern, butterflies, 1940s – 1950s, $20.00.
Old, butterflies, $30.00.
Modern, wisteria, 1930s – 1940s, $20.00.

*Noh mask,
modern,
$35.00.*

*Floral,
modern,
$25.00.*

*Butterfly,
modern,
$40.00.*

*Wisteria, old,
$45.00.*

*Iris, old,
$30.00.*

*Village scene,
old, $35.00.*

*Peonies,
modern,
$35.00.*

*Oriental let-
ters meaning
"happy," old,
$40.00.*

All these Satsuma buttons are medium, ranging in size from 1" to 1¼".

Seven Gods of Happiness

Traditionally the seven deities are worshiped throughout the year. According to legend, they arrive in a boat on the evening of December 31 to distribute luck and happiness to all mortals. The first few days of January are a special time in Japan, when thousands travel to shrines to worship. The deities are a part of everyday life; paintings, statues, and figurines are displayed in homes and businesses. If one worships one deity too much, he will be lacking in luck from the others.

Modern Satsuma buttons, medium, 1³/₁₆", late 1940s to early 1950s, unusual black background. Complete set, $350.00 – 425.00.

Row 1. Daikokuten, god of wealth.
Row 2. Bishamonten, god of dignity. Benzaiten, goddess of beauty.
Row 3. Ebisu, god of abundance. Hotei, god of happiness.
Row 4. Jurohjin, god of longevity. Fukurokuju, god of wisdom.

Arita is the name of a town in Japan on Kyushu Island. In the early 1600s, skilled potters from Korea were brought back to the town by Japanese warlords. The raw material kaolin from this mountainous region produces very fine white porcelain. To this day Arita is still known as the central point of Japan's finest porcelain. The first two buttons have the makers mark and the word JAPAN on the back. 1930s – 1950s.
$40.00; $60.00; $50.00.

In 1992 while reading an antiques trade paper, I came across a for-sale advertisement on Indian pottery buttons. Along with the 180 buttons I purchased was a letter telling the history behind these buttons. They were made in 1940 and 1941 by a woman from the Acoma Pueblo in New Mexico. Their original purpose was to be used on hand-made clothes, but due to World War II, this was never realized. Unfortunately, the card I had saved was stolen from under my table at a button show and I have only these three buttons left. $10.00 – 18.00 each.

Edward R. Taylor and his son, William H. Taylor, started the Ruskin Pottery Company in 1898 in Smethwick, England. In 1904 the firm started marking their wares with the name "Ruskin," taken from the famous writer, historian, and art critic, John Ruskin. This button represents the years of the Arts and Crafts movement when many people were rejecting the excessive ornamentation of the Victorian period. Simple, handmade furniture, jewelry, and decorative pieces were in style. The company stopped making items in 1933 after the death of William H. Taylor. Unfortunately along with him went the secrets of the glaze formula.

White body with blue-green glaze, covered with a clear glaze. Stamped into the back of the button is Ruskin, England. $25.00.

Three-piece multicolored enamel design on top of a separate ring of 28 cut steels. Cobalt blue enamel base, all three pieces held together by a heavy gilt wire that comes through the back by the shank, 1½". Large, $50.00.

Painted enamel landscape on silvered brass. Medium, $25.00.

Couple at table with dog resting on the floor, 1¼", $50.00.

Enamel set in a steel cup, 1⅜", $35.00.

Elephant. NBS medium, $20.00.

Champlevé enamel with hand-painted basket and flowers, 1⅛", $40.00 – 50.00.

Paris back, painted enamels.
Nut Tree Boy, 1¼", $150.00.
House and landscape, 1¼", $175.00.

Painted enamel on gilt brass with a rolled-over champlevé enamel border. Unusual painted design on this 1⁵/₁₆" button. Large, $40.00.

Woman wearing late eighteenth century costume, champlevé enamel, just over 1¼". $85.00.

All small buttons.
$12.00; $18.00; $10.00; $10.00; $10.00.

All medium buttons.
$18.00; $15.00; $20.00; $25.00.

All large buttons.
$30.00; $30.00; $35.00.

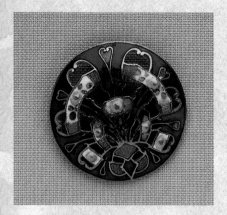

*Pierced enamel, just a hair shy
of 1⅛", $35.00.*

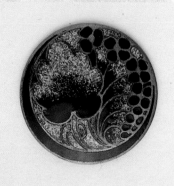

*Champlevé enamel from the Art
Nouveau period, $40.00.*

Pierced enamel, 1¼", $40.00.

*Stamped and pierced brass cham-
plevé enamel with 13 cut steels,
1¼", $45.00.*

*Pierced enamel with scalloped edge
and cut steel embellishment,
1³/₁₆", $45.00.*

*Good things come is small packages!
Painted enamel dog face surrounded
by cut steels, $40.00.*

Modern enamels, circa 1970s. $5.00 – 8.00 each.

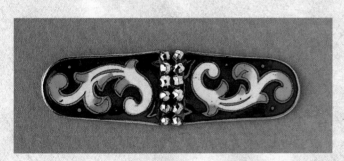

*Champlevé enamel with two rows of
cut steels, measures 1$^{15}/_{16}$" x $^9/_{16}$". I love
the shape. $30.00.*

*Dragonfly, pliqué a jour enamel by
studio button artist Nancy DuBois.
This type of enamel work is very hard
to make. $75.00.*

Fabric

Oriental woman, studio button, $8.00. Black beaded fabric, $8.00. Queen Elizabeth II, $15.00.
Reverse painted glass and rhinestone center, pad shank, $12.00. Anchor (Gone with the Wind), $8.00.
Garter (child's face), pad shank, $25.00. Crochet, with beaded paisley design, $8.00. Multicolored,
thread back, $10.00. Hand-stitched with pad shank, $10.00. Fabric mounted in metal, $18.00.

Pearlized clear glass buttons with a painted finish made from fish scales. I have been working on this tray for several years and enjoy finding odd shapes, realistics, sew-thrus, and ones with rhinestone embellishment. These range in size from ⅜" to 1⅛". Cat face, $15.00. Cat face with rhinestone eyes, $20.00. Gnome sitting under a toadstool, $18.00. All others, $2.00 – 6.00 each.

Mercury: Clear and colored glass buttons with gold and silver paint on the backside. Usually found with a self-shank, sew-thru, or cemented-on glass shank. Sizes shown are ¼" to 1⅛". Face, $12.00. Leaf, $7.00. Larger butterfly, $6.00. Red frosted glass with rhinestone center, $5.00. All others, $2.00 – 4.00 each.

Painted back: Clear glass with molded and paint-filled patterns on the back.
Sizes range from small to medium.
Sea life, $15.00. All others, $4.00 – 7.00 each.

Precision inlays: These modern buttons from the 1950s are not rare but are considered hard to find. Shown are examples in clear and colored glass, black glass, and one mounted in metal, with sizes ranging from small to medium.

The center star-shaped glass piece had to be cut just right so that it would fit correctly when glued to the inside of the base. The center piece is always flush with the top portion of the button. There is such little distinction between the two pieces that one must come to the conclusion that the last step in the process might have been to plane the surface of the button smooth.

Top center: Black glass mounted in metal, $25.00. Top right: Red faceted, $20.00. Center: Medium black glass, $25.00. Left: Small red sew-thru, $15.00. Bottom left: Black glass, $15.00. All others, $8.00 – 10.00 each.

Tingue: Red glass base with oblong flashed center, ⁹/₁₆", $85.00.

Victorian glass buttons, with four-way box and claw shanks, medium.
Gray incised glass, $8.00.
Sepia tinted milk glass, $20.00.
Caramel glass, $10.00.
Lavender glass, $18.00.
Light green glass, $12.00.

Old white glass with silvered brass bird escutcheon, 1³/₁₆",
$15.00 – 20.00.

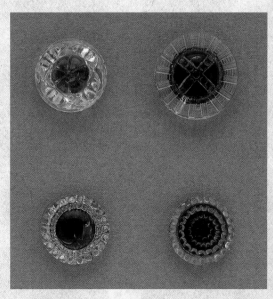

Radiants. Small, $12.00 – 16.00 each.

Vintage moonglows are inexpensive but still sought after by many collectors. These are more common designs, all NBS small. Lime colored, $6.00 each. All others, $3.00 – 5.00 each.

Vintage moonglows, medium size, ranging from ¹⁵/₁₆″ to 1¹/₁₆″, $7.00 – 12.00 each.

Vintage striped moonglows with smooth and textured tops.
Small, $5.00 – 8.00. Medium, $8.00 – 10.00.

New imported glass buttons, late 1990s.

Top left: White glass with aurora luster, metal loop shank and plate, 1⁹/₁₆", $7.00.

Top right: Clear glass with luster on backside, same shank as above, ¹¹/₁₆", $3.00.

Bottom: Egyptian head on tortoise glass, gold paint-filled lines, same shank as above, 1³/₈", $10.00.

An assortment of moonglows from the 1950s – 1960s. All are NBS small except where noted.

Clockwise from top: White with 12 colored stones, $12.00; white with two black enamel painted rings, $8.00; lady bug, $12.00; gray leaf, medium, $12.00; white with green paint, $10.00; blue rose with gold luster, $10.00; white molded top with seven colored rhinestones, $12.00; pink and white shave top, $8.00; white with 12 clear rhinestones, $10.00; white with three clear rhinestones, $6.00.

Center row: Aqua colored hat with three rhinestones on brim, $10.00; pink Princess Grace ring, $30.00; white molded top with 12 colored rhinestones, $15.00.

Men's vest buttons with rosette shanks, from the late 1800s to early 1900s. Notice the bottom row with the square, rhinestone, metallic paint finish with blue rhinestone, Star of David, and rounded top. $6.00 – 15.00 each.

Amethyst glass. Floral, $5.00. White glass and goldstone overlay, $5.00.

Cobalt blue glass: When held to the light, true cobalt buttons show a deep blue/purple color. Paisley, $5.00. Bird, $8.00.

Art Deco designs on opaque glass buttons, circa 1930s, medium and large, $5.00 − 8.00 each.

Frosted glass.
Top row left to right:
Sew-thru with silver luster.
Medium, $4.00. Embellished
with 12 rhinestones, and silver
luster. Large, $8.00 – 10.00.
Clear glass floral pattern, with
frosted background. Large, $6.00.

Bottom row, left to right:
Square with foil backed glass
insets. Medium, $5.00. Realistic
crown with gold luster. Medium,
$5.00. Floral. Medium, $2.00.

Opaque glass buttons with pictorial designs. Medium.
Racket, $12.00. Others, $4.00 – 8.00 each.

Poppers, a term collectors have used for years for Leo Popper & Sons, a glass company from New York, sold buttons from the 1870s to around 1917. Poppers have a very distinct look, and once examined they are easy to spot. The firm also manufactured black glass buttons and imported buttons from other countries. The buttons and assorted jewelry pieces were then sold to wholesalers and department stores. Shanks found on the above buttons are four-way box, loop shank and plate, key shank, and sew-thru. They measure from ³⁄₈" to 1³⁄₁₆". $4.00 – 12.00. Sew-thru, Large square, $25.00 – 35.00.

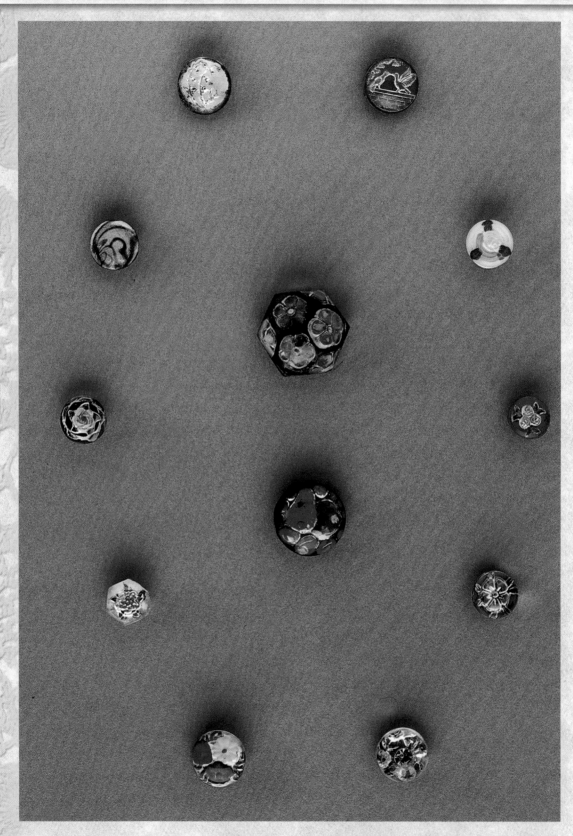

Many new collectors confuse two-piece cemented buttons, pictured here, with paperweight buttons. Paperweights are one-piece construction, and two-piece buttons have a separate glass shank cemented to a molded and paint-filled top. $4.00 – 8.00 each.

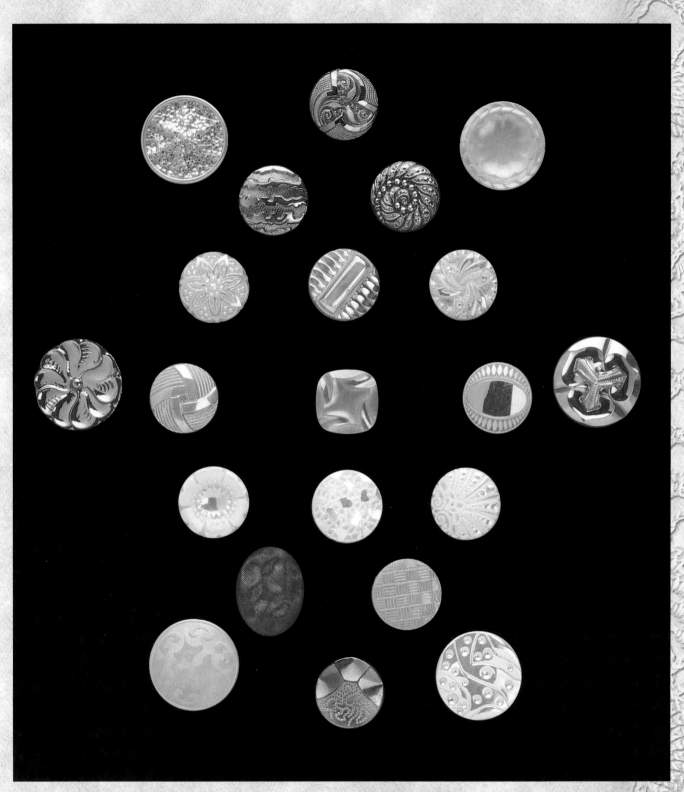

Aurora: These are among my favorites of the modern glass buttons. The coloring is fantastic, and they are still inexpensive. The majority have self-shanks, with sew-thrus and shapes being harder to find. Smalls, $4.00 each. Mediums, $6.00 – 8.00 each.

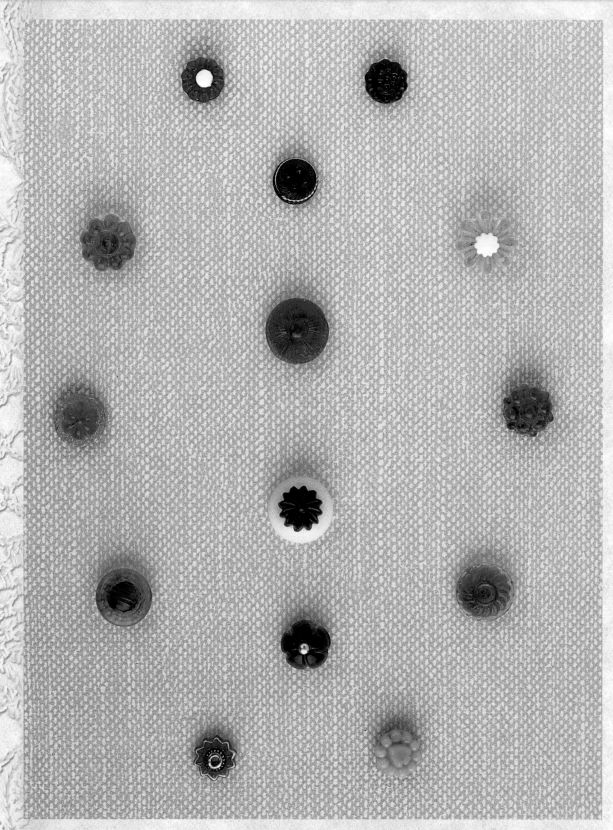

Charm string glass: This term is commonly used by collectors to describe the era of glass buttons from 1840 to the 1870s. Those shown have circular lines on the back caused by inserting and twisting the brass wire shank when the glass was still warm. Pictured are glass overlay, coronets, metal embedded, pin shank, and molded surface. Green with pin shank, $12.00. All others, $5.00 each.

Vintage lavender, tan, and gray moonglows, all small.

Leaf, $8.00. Gray with goldstone, $8.00. All others, $3.00 – 6.00 each.

*Old tortoise glass: Amber/brown glass
with brown irregular spots.*

Oblong, $4.00. Horseshoe design, $7.00.

*Lion's head molded
on clear glass with
iridescent luster, $10.00.*

"Kting" is the name Kathy Hoppe has given these buttons. They have a transparent glass base, flashed glass top, and are back-marked with the initial "K." Glass workers in the Czech Republic, who do special commissioned work for Kathy, made them this year. Several varied types of glass and different techniques were tried. An 85-year-old gentleman, who used to work in a German glass factory, was finally able to help them. There is no machining involved, only hands-on glasswork consisting of cutting, polishing, and cleaning of each button. These new buttons are very difficult and time consuming to make. $20.00 each.

New Kting-glows, moonglow base with flashed glass top, back marked with "K" initial. $22.00.

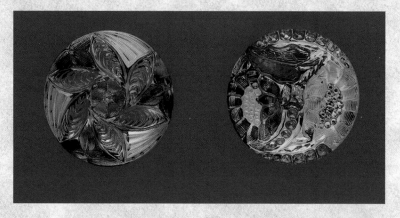

New clear lacy-type glass buttons, imported from the Czech Republic. Kathy painted the backs with semi-gloss acrylic enamel paint. The back is covered in black paint, and her initials "KH" are painted on. There were three different designs, and only 75 total painted buttons. $12.00.

New moonglow Christmas trees. Painted lights, $6.00.
Rhinestone lights, $7.50.

New moonglows, small and medium, $4.00 – 8.00 each.

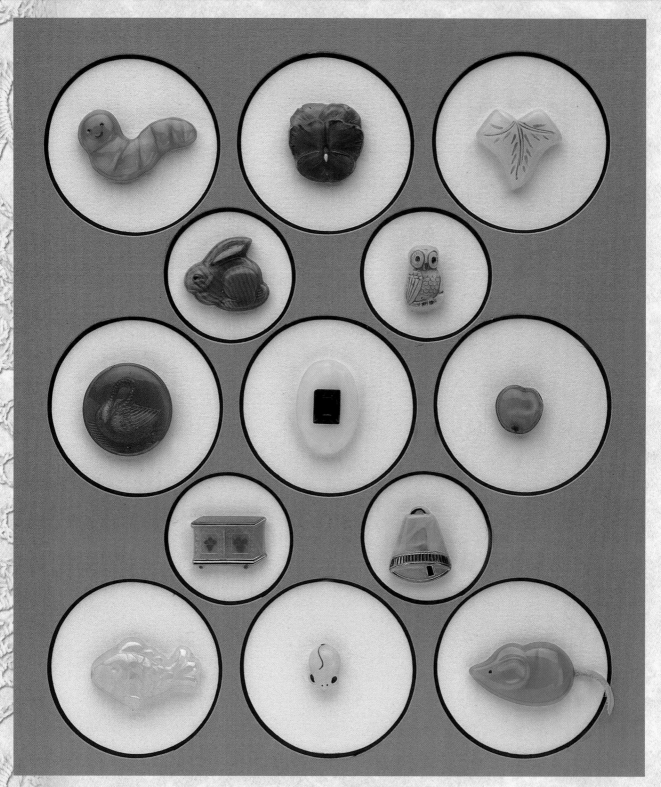

New Czech Republic moonglows, mid 1990s to present.

Center: Moonglow with precision inlay, $20.00.
All others, $4.00 – 7.00 each.

New Czech Republic moonglows, $4.00 – 10.00 each.

More New Czech Republic moonglows, $6.00 – 15.00 each.

Opaque glass buttons, late 1940s to early 1960s. Hat box, $10.00. Others, $3.00 – 6.00 each.

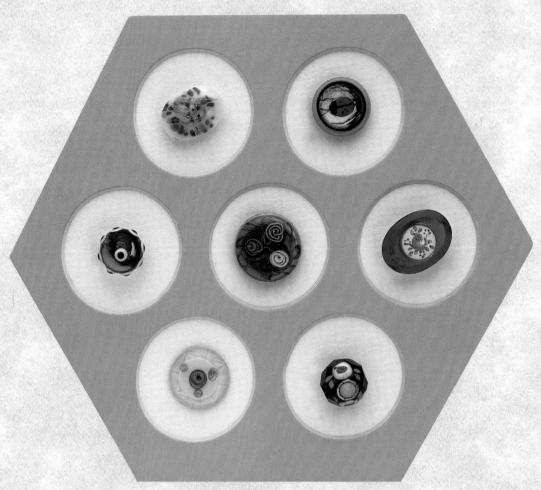

An assortment of glass buttons, including glass in glass and glass overlay, $7.00 – 12.00 each.

Vintage pierced glass buttons from ¼" to 1¹⁄₁₆". $8.00 – 15.00 each.

A colorful Bimini glass button made of various shades of blue, enhanced with gold paint. It has the typical large brass shank plate and loop. This one is marked Made in England and has the potted tree mark, although there are Bimini types that are not marked. Circa 1940s. $8.00.

Large transparent green/blue glass button with shelf-shank. The birds, branch, and flowers are painted in both gold and silver luster. $15.00 – 20.00.

Cabochon set in a faceted transparent green glass base with a four-way metal box shank, ⁷/₈" x 1⁷/₁₆", $22.00.

Pink glass with gold luster finish, 1¹/₁₆", 1950s, $8.00.

Clear glass button with silver pearlized paint. This button definitely has something to do with rail transportation. $7.00 – 10.00.

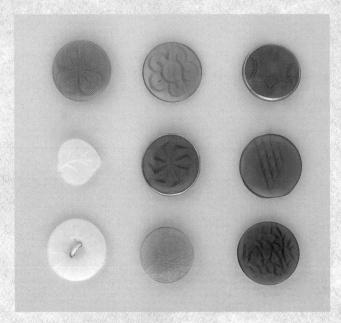

DUGS (design under glass surface), late 1940s to early 1950s. $4.00 – 7.00 each.

Old red glass buttons, pre-1918. $4.00 – 10.00 each.

Fun mountings.
Same buttons in different colors. Circa 1930s to early 1960s.
Row 1: Faceted opaque glass with silver luster. $4.00.
Row 2: Molded opaque glass with aurora luster. $4.00.
Row 3: Opaque glass sew-thru with gold luster. $4.00.
Row 4: Candy striped moonglow butterflies. $15.00.
Row 5: Transparent glass sew-thrus. $4.00.
Row 6: Faceted moonglows with gold luster. $5.00.
Row 7: Transparent glass sew-thrus. $3.00.

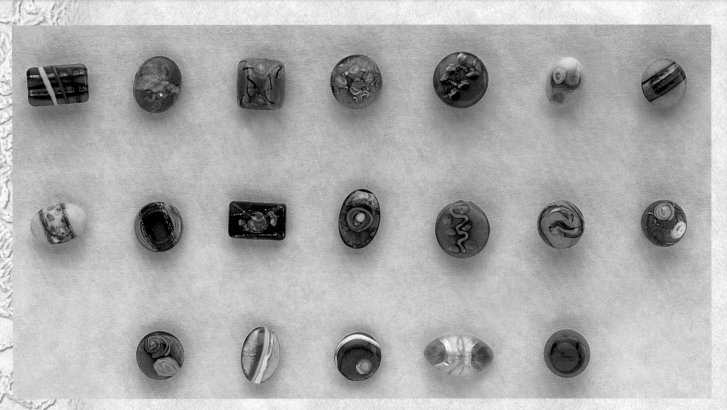

Several of these were in my first book, but I just love diminutives and small glass buttons. All have the four-way metal box shank, and some have thread grooves. Their make-up includes goldstone, glass overlay, and embedded foil; the bottom right button is what collectors call a peacock eye.
Peacock eye, diminutive, $25.00. All others, $5.00 – 10.00 each.

At first glance, I thought this was a china button. On closer inspection, I found it was molded and painted white glass. Due to the large sew-thru holes, I am assuming it was worn on a child's undergarment. NBS small, $10.00.

Antiquarians have glass hanging down between U shank (see detail photo). $5.00 – 10.00.

Metals

Damascene is made by inlaying gold/silver wire or shapes into blackened iron or steel.
Fan, backmarked JAPAN, $18.00
Oval with butterflies, $10.00.

Hard white pewter buttons, circa 1810 – 1830.
Left: Backmarked G. Smiths Manufacture, pewter hump with copper wire shank, $22.00.
Right: Backmarked H. Smiths Manufacture, pewter hump with brass wire shank, $20.00.

Back view of two cricket cages.

Cricket cages, pierced/openwork metal buttons with backs that are divided into segments. Some have a single soldered-on shank, while others consist of two halves pushed together to form the shank. $3.00 – 10.00.

85

This type of "Japanned brass" buttons is inexpensive, but it is still fun to see how many different designs one can accumulate. $6.00 – 8.00.

Stenciled disc under a separate brass rim, steel back and wire loop shank, ¹¹/₁₆". $5.00 and $8.00.

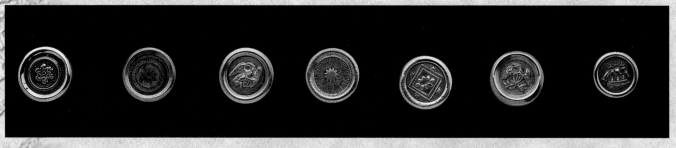

True Jacksonians are pictorials, while their cousins have conventional designs. They are small buttons with a separate rim that is usually plain. Decorative rims on true Jacksonians are very rare.

| $6.00 | $6.00 | $30.00 | $6.00 | $6.00 | $35.00 | $40.00 |

French metals were manufactured in France during the 1930s and 1940s. Many are copies of old picture buttons while others are original designs. The majority are medium and large size and may include embellishments such as enamel and paste. French metals are lighter in weight than their older counterparts and discolor easily. They can be a dramatic addition to any tray, especially for subjects that are hard to find on old buttons. These measure 1 7/16" to 2".

Kittens at play, $35.00. Cat, $40.00. Child's face, $25.00. Owl, $45.00.

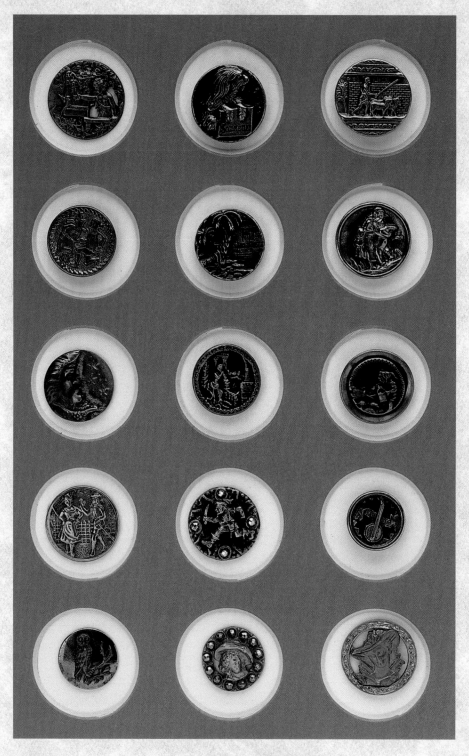

Old picture buttons, small.

Woman at window, $7.00.	Dog holding card, souvenir, $20.00.	Shepherd, $4.00.
Dancing couple, $5.00.	Palm trees, buildings, $4.00.	Baby's first step, $8.00.
Sol and Luna, $6.00.	Girl on castle terrace, $7.00.	Gnome, $12.00.
Maude Miller, $8.00.	The Giant, $12.00.	Banjo, $6.00.
Owl, $7.00.	Duchess of Devonshire, $10.00.	Pretty woman, $8.00.

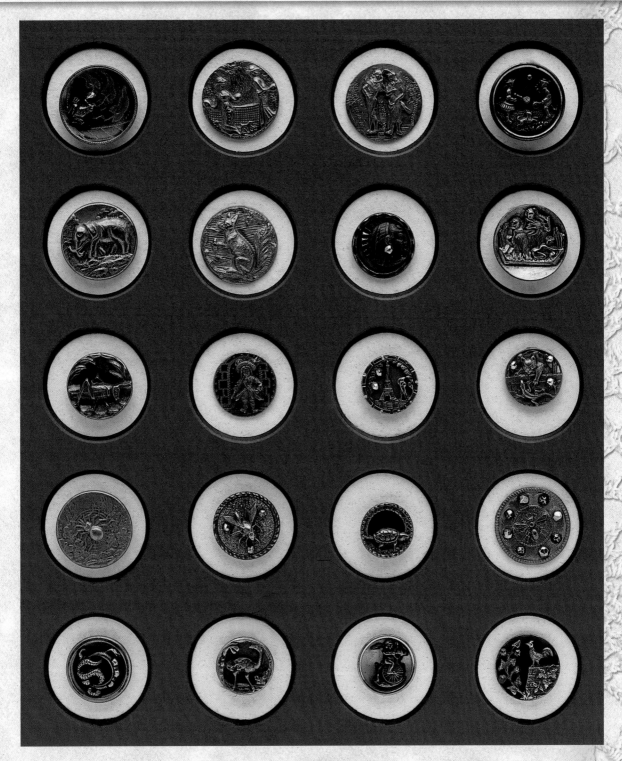

Old picture buttons, small.

Frog, $15.00.
Elephant, $12.00.
Grasshopper, $9.00.
Spider, $10.00.
Snake, $12.00.

Tennis, $10.00.
Squirrel, $7.00.
Little colonel, $12.00.
Mosquito, $7.00.
Ostrich, $12.00.

Fops, $12.00.
Egyptian $10.00.
Eiffel Tower, $20.00.
Turtle, $12.00.
Cupid, $10.00.

Children, $15.00.
Putti, $10.00.
Cat, $15.00.
Bee, $8.00.
Rooster, $15.00.

Old picture buttons, small.

Basket, $7.00.

Girl, $7.00.

Train, $6.00.

Butterfly, $6.00.

Club, w/glass, $6.00.

Train under bridge, $7.00.

Boy on wall, $10.00.

Ships, crystallized tin, $7.00.

Bull fight, $12.00.

At the Inn, $10.00.

Dog, steel cup, $9.00.

Girl by fence, $9.00.

Little Nemo, $7.00.

Lyre, cut steel, $6.00.

Horse and jockey, $15.00.

Old picture buttons, small.

Egyptian, $7.00.	Owl, $9.00.	Dragon, original tint, $5.00.
Hunting dog, $5.00.	Mother feeding babies, $6.00.	Salamander, $6.00.
Ewer, $6.00.	Woman's head, $6.00.	Dog, cut steels, $12.00.
Pyramid, $10.00.	Spider, $12.00.	Nekhbet, vulture goddess, $8.00.
Fly, $7.00.	Fish, pole, net, $8.00.	Cabbage baby, $10.00.

Small pewter buttons are still plentiful. They do not respond to a magnet, are lighter in weight than other metals, and are easily scratched. The fun part is finding the pictorial ones.

Old pewter buttons.

Pattern, $2.00.	*Owl, $6.00.*	*Floral, $3.00.*
Pattern, $3.00.	*Peacock, $8.00.*	*Patterns, $3.00.*
Insect, $6.00.	*Riding a toboggan, $10.00.*	*Wheat, scythe, $4.00.*
Pattern, $3.00.	*Butterfly, $6.00.*	*Floral, $3.00.*
Floral, ball shape, $5.00.	*Owl, moon, and star, $7.00.*	*Anchor, $4.00.*

Old pewter buttons.

Basket, medium, $8.00.	Lion, medium, $18.00.	Buckle, pierced, medium, $10.00.
Floral, large, $8.00.	Swan, large, $25.00.	Floral, large, $10.00.
Floral, large, $8.00.	Snake, medium, $20.00.	Floral, very large, $10.00.
Floral, medium, $8.00.		Wheat and scythe, medium, $10.00.

*Frog sitting on a toadstool.
Medium, $15.00.*

*Under the sea, one-piece stamped
brass seahorse, crab, fish, and
shells, Nice detail.
Medium, $18.00.*

*Polar bear with flag, one of
several buttons made in
recognition of Admiral Peary's
trip to the North Pole.
Medium, $20.00.*

*Teddy Roosevelt, hunting trip,
stamped one-piece brass.
Medium, $40.00.*

*Giraffe, nice harder-to-find subject for an
animal tray, original painted background.
1¹¹/₁₆". Large, $60.00.*

Lizard on fence. 1½". Large, $35.00.

*Cat on roof, white metal,
steel liner, set in brass,
1¹/₁₆", $30.00.*

*Elephant, stamped one-piece
brass, 1³/₁₆", $20.00.*

Rarin' to go, 1⁷/₁₆". $25.00.

*Tally ho, stamped one-piece brass,
1⁹/₁₆", $32.00.*

*All saddled up, fabulous detail, 1⁷/₁₆".
$45.00 – 60.00.*

*Buck in woods, stamped brass
surrounded by a white metal
collet. Medium, $18.00.*

St. Hubert's Hounds, the center escutcheon holds a steel ring in place against the brass back, 1⁹/₁₆", $40.00.

Fox and the stork, stamped brass, 1³/₈", $35.00.

Dogs attacking a boar. Medium, $15.00.

Rampant lion, pierced brass with 16 cut steels, 1³/₄", $35.00.

Fox and the grapes, stamped brass with original red tint, 1³/₈", $35.00.

Flying ducks, cattails, 1¹¹⁄₁₆".
$20.00.

Timid owl, brass with steel and black
lacquered steel back. Medium, $15.00.

Eagle, black painted background,
1³⁄₈", $18.00.

Bird on a trellis.
Medium, $15.00.

Crane, stamped brass design backed
by wood, painted steel back
and loop shank. 1³⁄₈", $18.00.

Tree creepers, stamped brass design,
steel liner, 1⁷⁄₁₆". $20.00.

Owl on branch, pewter owl applied to concave one-piece brass with original red tint, 1½", $38.00.

Owl's face, stamped brass with faceted steels for eyes, fastened by two wires to a steel back. Medium, $18.00.

Rooster. Medium, $20.00.

Game birds, raised stamped brass center over a steel liner, separate brass rim. 1⅞", $22.00.

Birds under umbrella, 1¾". $35.00.

Beetle, brown tinted brass with steel rim, 1⁷/₁₆", $18.00.

Swallow in the chimney, heavy one-piece stamped brass, large cut steels around border and a tiny cut steel for the bird's eye, 1¹¹/₁₆", $40.00.

Butterfly with wood background. Large, $20.00.

Wasp (long narrow waist and posterior) by a strawberry vine. Design is attached to a textured background with four cut steels. 1¼", $22.00.

Pewter hornet or wasp escutcheon in a white metal cup. Medium, $12.00.

Pot of basil sitting on a terrace wall, with white metal building scene in background, 1⁷⁄₁₆", $20.00.

Bridge scene with castle on the left. Stamped and tinted brass, black lacquered back and wire shank. Large, $18.00.

Medieval village, 1½", $20.00.

Pavilion, stamped and tinted brass, narrow white metal border, 1⁵⁄₁₆", $18.00.

Ancient ruins, common. Medium, $12.00.

Eiffel Tower, stamped brass, cut steel embellishment and pearl background set in a steel cup, 1¹⁄₁₆", $45.00 – 60.00.

Cherub riding a seahorse, stamped and tinted brass with white metal rim. Large, $30.00.

Cupid in danger, stamped center with steel liner under a decorative brass rim, 1⁷/₁₆", $25.00.

Cherub riding a robin. Stamped and tinted brass over a black painted background with a white metal rim. Large, $18.00.

Over the wall, stamped brass with original blue tint on brick wall. Black lacquered steel back and a wire shank, 1¼", $30.00.

Cupid under umbrella and sitting on a grape vine. Stamped and tinted brass. Large, $35.00.

Cherub on crescent.
Medium, $20.00.

Cherub and birds, 1⁵⁄₁₆", $20.00.

Putti riding a goat, stamped
and tinted brass, 1⅛", $25.00.

Ariel, pewter center design
has lost most of the original
red tint, 1", $18.00.

Cupid and Venus, pierced
one-piece brass,
1¹⁄₁₆", $18.00.

Shaking the apple tree, 1¼", stamped and tinted brass with black lacquered steel back and loop shank. $38.00.

Mademoiselle at the well, stamped and tinted brass. 1⁵⁄₁₆", $22.00.

Kate Greenaway — Little Miss Patty and Master Paul, stamped brass, black lacquered steel back and loop shank. 1⁷⁄₁₆", $85.00 – 100.00.

Kate Greenaway — See-Saw Jack, painted pewter center design, painted metal background, brass rim. 1⁹⁄₁₆", $150.00 – 200.00.

Porridge time, stamped center design over a textured brass background, set in a steel cup, 1³⁄₈", $150.00.

Daydreaming stamped and tinted brass. 1⅛", $25.00.

Goethe's farewell to Frederica,
1½", $25.00.

Woodland vows, 1⁷⁄₁₆".
$22.00.

Lovers, stamped openwork brass, 1⁹⁄₁₆",
$25.00.

Love's service, stamped and lustered
brass, 1⁷⁄₁₆", $35.00.

French Fop, one-piece stamped brass,
1⁷⁄₁₆", $55.00.

Incroyable and Merveilleuse (incredi-
ble and marvelous), 1½", $55.00.

Grand Canal in Venice, lady with
parasol in gondola, stamped brass,
black lacquered back with loop shank,
1¹⁄₁₆", $18.00.

Lovers with birdcage, two-piece brass,
backmarked EINGETR.MUSTER
W.L.R.. NBS large, $28.00.

Egyptian head, 1⁵⁄₁₆", $28.00.

Funeral mask, stamped brass with
black lacquered steel back and loop
shank. NBS large, $22.00.

Cleopatra playing a harp, fantastic detail on
this 1⁷⁄₁₆" button. It has a bar shank on the back
marked L.F. Depose. $50.00.

Large stamped brass and cut steel piece, attached to a decorative back. Fabulous animal button, $1^{11}/_{16}$", $25.00.

Mask, brass over screen, with a shiny steel background showing through. White metal rim with black lacquered steel back and wire shank, $1^3/_8$". $15.00.

Snail on a sea serpent. Medium, $10.00.

Volcano and crescent moon with blue tinted cut steels. Possibly Mont Pelée in Martinique which erupted in 1902, killing 38,000 people. One-piece silvered brass, 1". $18.00 – 22.00.

The Peasant of the Danube, has also been called Rip Van Winkle, 1½", $35.00.

Henry of Navarre, stamped and pierced brass, 1⁷⁄₁₆", $45.00.

Gentleman in eighteenth century costume, a one-piece brass button with finely engraved ground, birds, flowers, and tiny cut steel blossoms. 1⁷⁄₁₆", $50.00 – 60.00.

Jousting, one-piece stamped brass, fabulous three-dimensional details, shields all around the border. 1⁵⁄₈", $45.00 – 55.00.

Gladiators, one-piece stamped pierced brass with cut steels, fabulous detail. 1⁹⁄₁₆", $50.00.

Pied Piper of Hamlin: A different version than the one you normally see. Silvered brass center with brass rim. Large, $35.00.

The Kill, purple tinted stamped brass, painted background, 1½", $30.00.

Landsknechts were sixteenth century German soldiers, who later became mercenaries for hire. This button depicts the typical clothing and breastplate they would have worn, 1⁷⁄₁₆", $30.00.

King George VI reigned England from 1936 to 1952. In 1938, he visited France, and in 1939 he went to Canada and the United States. One-piece silvered brass button, circa 1939, back-marked Pairstyle. 1³⁄₈", $25.00.

Fernando Francisco De Avalos, stamped brass design over a steel liner and painted background, 1½", $35.00.

The Trumpeter of Cracow, even in this large size is one of the most common picture buttons. Pewter design over a painted background, brass rim, $12.00.

Fall of Granada, stamped brass center with purple tint, painted black background. Thin steel liner, black lacquered back and wire shank. Large, 1⁷⁄₁₆", $30.00.

Knights of the Holy Grail, stamped and tinted brass, 1⅛", $20.00.

Blacksmith Shop, bronze tinted stamped brass, 1¼", $30.00.

Frederick Barbarossa, stamped and pierced brass over a steel mirror background, black lacquered back and wire loop shank, hair over, 1⁵⁄₁₆", $25.00.

Herald on horseback, 1⁹⁄₁₆", $35.00.

Known as Charles V, sixteenth century. NBS medium, $25.00.

Swiss Hunter, stamped brass over a dark colored wood background, 1½", $30.00.

The Trumpeter of Sackingen, stamped brass
with a cut-out for a white metal full moon. A
huge 1⅞" with lots of detail, $75.00 – 90.00.

Knight with shield and spiked weapon
called a mace. Stamped and tinted brass
with white metal rim, 1⁹⁄₁₆", $20.00.

King Arthur, one-piece stamped
brass with bar shank, 1⅜", $30.00.

In the past this button has been called Lohengrin and
King Harold. In About Buttons by Peggy Ann
Osborne, she makes reference to the Norse god Odin.
Odhinn, Woden, Wotan, and Wuotan are different
language variations of this highest god of the Norse
people. One-piece stamped brass with cut steel
embellishments, 1⁵⁄₁₆", $35.00.

Pax (Peace), one-piece stamped silvered brass. There is also a companion button called Bellum (War). 1¹³/₁₆", $85.00.

Medea, stamped and tinted brass over wood background, 1⁵/₈", $30.00.

Jupiter and Minerva, brass center over a wood background, 1⁹/₁₆", $22.00.

Lion's head. Medium, $12.00.

Thor, god of thunder and son of Odin, pictured with his hammer or ax, which returns to him when thrown. Stamped brass over a wood background, 1⁹/₁₆", $22.00.

Aeneas, the Trojan prince. Large, $15.00.

St. George slaying the dragon, stamped brass, black painted background, 1⁵/₁₆", $18.00.

Hippolyta, queen of the Amazons, 1¼", $28.00.

*Mikado in the Garden, brass,
1⁷⁄₁₆". $30.00.*

*Genghis Kahn, stamped and tinted
brass, loop shank. 1⁷⁄₁₆", $28.00.*

*Heron and Japanese home on
one-piece openwork brass with
cut steels and loop shank.
1¼", $20.00.*

*Oriental fable, concave,
one-piece brass.
Medium, $12.00.*

*Samurai warrior,
one-piece stamped and
silvered brass with added
gilding. Medium, $12.00.*

*Oriental lady with fan,
one-piece stamped and pierced
brass. 1¹⁄₁₆", $15.00.*

Persian Lindworm Slayer, my interpretation of the button we know as Chinese Dragon Slayer. Stamped brass over a rush basket weave pattern, 1½". $25.00.

1 ⅜", wood background, $22.00.

Oriental Wedding, one-piece pierced brass with cut steel embellishment, 1 ⁹⁄₁₆". $38.00.

1⅝", one-piece brass with cut steels. Probably a rendition of one of the characters from Gilbert & Sullivan's The Mikado. $35.00.

Known as Yum-Yum from The Mikado. 1 ⅜". $20.00.

Kaguya Hime, the bamboo princess. ¹⁵⁄₁₆", $8.00.

Four-leaf clover with a snake wrapped around the stem and a tiny butterfly off to the right, embellished wth cut steels. Large, 1¼", $20.00.

Iris on pierced brass with enamel embellishment. Large, $35.00.

Stamped brass leaf, wood background, decorative white metal liner, mounted in brass, 1½", $18.00.

Aster on trellis, modified square with four cut steel pieces, back-marked T.W. & W., HM, Paris Brevete, 1³⁄₁₆", $18.00.

Potted palm, one-piece brass. Medium, $10.00.

The angel Gabriel. There are different variations of this button, but I especially like the decorative rim on this one. Large, $30.00.

St. Cecilia. Original black painted background, scarce, especially in this condition. Just under 1³/₄", $100.00 – 125.00.

Moses found in the bullrushes by the king's daughter while Miriam, his sister, looks on. One-piece openwork brass, 1⁷/₁₆". $125.00.

Eliezer at the well. This is another religious button that has several variations. This example gives the illusion of a separate design and rim when it is really one piece with a steel and black lacquered back. 1½", $25.00.

Lady standing by a shield, dressed in late fifteenth century clothing. One-piece pierced brass. 1⁷/₁₆", $38.00.

Holy Fair. This button has had this title for quite some time, taken from a poem written by Robert Burns. I have read and reread different versions of Holy Fair but do not see any correlation. 1⁷/₁₆", $32.00.

Empress Theodora served at the side of her husband Emperor Justinian. During a political revolt in 532 A.D. at the Hippodrome, she convinced her husband to stand and fight for his throne. Stamped and tinted brass with pierced holes in her crown and breastplate that reveal a steel backing. 1³/₈", $30.00.

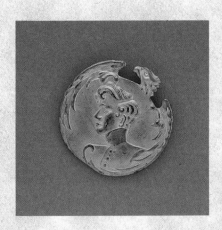

Sarah Bernhardt as L'Aiglon, heavily gilded, 1". $22.00.

Two very large metal buttons depicting Queen Elizabeth II. They have a bronze colored finish and were made for her coronation in 1953. $20.00 – 25.00 each.

*Pretty woman of two-piece brass. The stamping of her bust fits into notches in the back circle, loop shank and plate, 1 1/16".
$18.00.*

Frances Folsom-Preston, former wife of President Glover Cleveland, the first and only couple married in the White House. Married in the Blue Room on June 2, 1886, he was 49 and she was 22. Frances was the daughter of Cleveland's previous law partner and friend, Oscar Folsom. 1 7/8". $75.00 – 90.00.

Wine flagon and flowers, stamped and tinted brass over a wood background. Blackened liner and rim, loop shank. 1⁷⁄₁₆", $18.00.

Basket filled with flowers with a garden hat beside it. Heavily tinted brass top that extends over the edges and attaches to a self-shanked brass back. 1½", $20.00.

Potted flowers on a stylistic shield, stamped brass with a purple tint. 1⁷⁄₁₆", $10.00.

Basket of flowers, handle continues around the rim. Textured background and a thin shiny liner. 1¼", $12.00.

Large framed cut-steel piece representing a mirror surrounded by a floral garland. Tinted background set in a steel cup. 1¼", $20.00.

Lady's hat, two-piece hollow brass with vent holes and heavy loop shank. 1", $10.00.

Relaxing at the Inn, picturing a violinist, woman, and man having a drink, ¹⁵/₁₆", $10.00.

Ship of devilment, white metal front wrapped around a shelf-shank brass back, 1¼", $12.00.

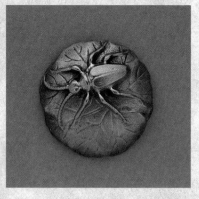

Beetle, one-piece stamped brass. Medium, $10.00.

Oriental women on pattens. Stamped and pierced brass. 1¹/₁₆", $10.00.

The Reaper, stamped and tooled background with a separate brass rim, wire loop shank, 1³/₁₆", $15.00 – 20.00 each.

Ducks on pond, one-piece stamped brass with cut steel ducks. 1⁷⁄₁₆", $30.00.

Rooster head, one-piece stamped brass. 1¹³⁄₁₆", $40.00.

Gnomes carrying lilies-of-the-valley, stamped and tinted brass. Black lacquered steel back and loop shank, 1½". $60.00.

Stamped brass whippet's head, fastened to one-piece brass. Cut steels embellish the border, eye, whip, and collar. A high quality button that measures 2". $125.00 – 150.00.

Since the early 1300s the British have been hallmarking items made of silver or gold. As far as British silver buttons go, the majority of marks will date the buttons from the 1870s – 1910s.

The maker's mark is the initials of the person who made the item or the person who submitted it to the assay office. Assay office marks may include the following, either a lion's head for London; three castles for Edinburgh; a tree, a fish, and a bird for Glasgow; an anchor for Birmingham; a crown for Sheffield; or three sheaves of corn for Chester. The quality of the silver is usually 92.5% pure silver and will be marked with a lion with one paw raised, facing left. The date mark will be either an upper or lower case letter. The duty mark found on some pieces was one of the heads of the reigning monarch and proof that taxes were paid.

Hallmarks on this set denote the following: Birmingham, 1902, and the initials L & S, for Levi and Salaman. The partnership of Phineas Levi and Joseph Salaman produced items such as jewelry, perfume holders, purses, and other novelty items. This beautiful boxed set consists of six matching buttons, a buckle, and two shoe buckles depicting a fabulous animal. $600.00 – 800.00.

Taxco, Mexico, is well-known for its production of silver and for the many artists who live and work there. From the 1930s – 1960s, designers like Los Castillo, Hector Aguilar, and American William Spratling, produced some of the finest and most sought-after Mexican jewelery and wares. The workshops employed many of the local people which gave a great boost to the area's economy. After years of training, several silversmiths went on to open their own shops. Most collectors prefer the signed Taxco pieces, but there are also many quality pieces that are unsigned.

Clockwise from top left:

Flower 1¼", signed Silver and Mexico, $25.00. Smaller version of same flower, unsigned, ¹⁵⁄₁₆", $15.00. Oval blossom, 1⁵⁄₁₆", signed Sterling, Los Castillo, Taxco, 104 (design number), Made in Mexico, $50.00. Round with eight-point star, ¾", signed Sterling Mexico, $20.00. Round, high-domed with stamped pattern and copper shank, just shy of ⅞", unsigned, $10.00. Round with stamped pattern, 1⅛", with long silver shank, unsigned, $12.00. Copper swan on brass, 1⁷⁄₁₆", signed Moya and Mexico, $30.00. Shell-shaped with simple lines, unmarked, ¹³⁄₁₆", $10.00. Dome center with rope border, ¾", signed Taxco, 980 (silver content) and the initials RD in a circle (Rafael Dominguez), 1940s or 1950s, $25.00. Sleeping man, ⅞" x 1", signed Mexico Silver, $20.00.

Center:

Dome with stylized border, 1", signed Taxco 980, $25.00. Square with four-leaf clover, ⅞", signed Sterling and Taxco, $20.00.

*What's the story behind this button?
Swan on a pond with stairs that lead
up to an archway. Stamped brass with
steel background, black lacquered back
and wire shank. 1¹⁄₁₆", $20.00.*

"Steel cup" buttons, large.

Top row, left to right:

*Wood under tinted steel, set in a blue
tinted cup, $18.00.
Stamped brass dragon head on a wood
background with cut steels, $22.00.*

Bottom row, left to right:

*Pearl center, $22.00.
Brass and cut steel embellishment in a
blue tinted cup, $18.00.*

*Third Avenue silver buttons,
probably German silver, were made in
the early 1900s. All are back marked
Knopfkonig Graz, which means
Button King. The top button
portrays Friedrich Ludwig Jahn
(1778 – 1852), founder of the
turnverein, a gymnastics club.
$20.00 – 25.00 each.*

*The Wounded Cuirassier, back-marked
T.W. & W., HM, Paris Breveté
S.G.D. G., 1¼", $35.00.*

*Gem tintypes were made of japanned tin
which was coated and then dipped in silver
nitrate. The picture had to be taken and
developed in the camera before the chemicals
dried. Once the picture was done, it was
coated with varnish for preservation, then
cut out with tin snips and mounted in
jewelry and buttons. Larger tintypes or
ferrotypes can be found in old family albums.
1850s – 1920s.
Small, $20.00. Medium, $35.00.*

*Metal stencils are still inexpensive.
The trick is finding them with
no fading or chipped paint, 1930s.
⁹⁄₁₆" – ¹¹⁄₁₆". $5.00 – 7.00 each.*

*Painting on ivory under glass,
$1^5/_{16}$", $300.00.*

Young woman, $1^5/_{16}$", $18.00.

*Tennis anyone? Stamped one-piece
brass, just over 1", $18.00.*

*Hercules wrestling the Nemean Lion, stamped
brass, black lacquered steel back and wire loop
shank, $1^1/_{16}$", $20.00.*

*Ko-Ko from the Mikado,
$1^1/_2$", $20.00.*

*Simple Simon, lacking in quality.
Medium, $15.00.*

While doing a little research for this boxed set of buttons, I ran across some interesting facts and background history. Charles Tobias, CEO of Pussers West Indies, which has stores and restaurants in the British Virgin Isles, commissioned this set in recognition of Vice-Admiral Horatio Nelson. Pussers is well-known for its production of British Navy Pussers Rum.

Nelson is considered the most famous admiral of his time. At the age of 12, he was a midshipman, and by 14, he was navigating a ship through the Northwest Passage. Nelson climbed the ranks by leading and winning battle after battle. In 1787 he married Frances Nesbit, but that was not to last, and the marriage ended in 1801. Nelson had an affair with Emma Hamilton, who was the wife of Sir William Hamilton, the British Ambassador of Naples and one of Nelson's best friends. Hamilton was much older than Emma and tolerated her affair with Nelson. After Nelson's divorce, he purchased a home and the three of them peacefully coexisted. Nelson and his mistress never married, but they had a daughter together named Horatia.

From 1655 to 1970, the Royal Navy gave their ships' crews a daily ration of rum and double amounts before going into action. When the tradition was first started, they received straight rum, but as the years passed, the rum was mixed with different quantities of water, a mixture known as grog. In 1970, the Royal Navy stopped the issue of daily rum.

Tobias is vice-president of the Friends of the National Maritime Museum. The museum houses a large collection of Nelson memorabilia, including the original tunic Nelson was wearing when he died from wounds received in the Battle of Trafalgar. Tobias was given special permission to have molds made from the buttons on this tunic. Twelve years ago a firm in London made 1,000 sets for him, and he sold them in Pussers Company Store for $100.00 per set. His firm still sells the famous British Navy Pussers Rum.

Commissioned boxed set, gold plated to seven microns. Back-marked London, Nelson, 1797, and pictures a partial anchor on back.
$250.00 – 300.00.

Metals

Daniel Baughman studied sculpture and printmaking at Illinois Wesleyan University. In 1976, he started Battersea Buttons, a division of Bergamot Brass Works, Inc. He came up with the name while on a trip to England seeking old molds for his pewter buttons. From 1976 to 1980, the company produced buttons for the retail market in pewter, many with brass or copper plating, and solid fine pewter. During this time, Battersea also made buttons for corporations to give to their employees. Battersea pewter buttons from 1976 to 1980 have a regular self-shank. The fine pewter buttons from this same period have a patented facial shank, taken from Baughman's likeness.

A decision was made to stop production due to high cost and lack of market acceptance by retail stores. His attention was redirected toward the production of statues, buckles, key tags, and Christmas ornaments. Buttons produced from 1976 to 1980 are no longer available through Battersea. The molds have been destroyed.

When Baughman met his wife Kathy, he eventually showed her the buttons. She was fascinated with them. In 1995, under Kathy's direction, Battersea was again producing buttons while Daniel continued the day-to-day operations of the company. Each year's set comes on a beautiful display card.

All the button sets they have produced since 1995 have the facial shanks. The five-piece 1997 set, Alice in Wonderland, has the face of their daughter, Bryn Alice, on the shank. Battersea buttons are also available as singles and come in various metals and finishes including fine pewter, bronze, silver and gold plate, and sterling silver plate. A major plus for collectors are the limited quantities produced. Since 1995, only 400 to 500 of each button have been made. In 1999, Battersea started making a special annual Christmas button.

2000 collection, Native American set: Fine pewter, silver plated, with patented facial shank. $140.00.

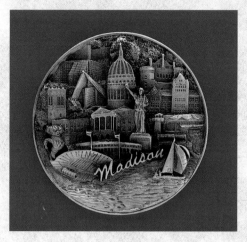

Battersea made this fabulous button for the 1997 National Button Society Show, held in Wisconsin. It was strictly limited to 500 buttons and is already highly collectible. The detail is exceptional, and it is one of my favorite National buttons. Large, $65.00 – 75.00.

Pansy Face, with facial shank, back-marked Battersea Pewter and Battersea Ltd. 1978, $20.00.
Charles the First of England, back-marked Battersea Pewter, Battersea Ltd., with facial shank. Diminutive, $7.00.
Art Nouveau Woman, back-marked Battersea Ltd., 1976, no facial shank. $25.00.

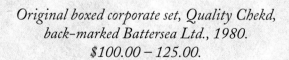

Original boxed corporate set, Quality Chekd, back-marked Battersea Ltd., 1980. $100.00 – 125.00.

Assorted silver buttons, sizes from ⁷⁄₁₆" to 1".
Row 1: Ship, hallmarked S.B. L. (Samuel Boyce Landeck, importer of German and Dutch goods),
F (mark for imported goods between 1867 – 1904), crown (town mark for Sheffield), lion (stands
for .925 sterling), f (Sheffield date-letter for 1898), $45.00. Coin type, R &W (Reynolds & Webster),
Birmingham, 1904, $30.00. Art Nouveau woman's head, HM (Henry Matthews),
Birmingham, 1901, $35.00.
Row 2: Flower, gold wash center, marked Silver, $18.00. Mask, marked Peru, 925, JT, $20.00.
Row 3: Head, marked 925, $22.00. Head, marked 925 and MEX, $25.00.
Row 4: Filigree, marked 930S, date unknown, $15.00. Fish, marked Sterling, $8.00.

Harrison and Morton, 23rd President and Vice President of the United States, 1889 – 1893. Heavily tinted steel front, black lacquered steel back with loop shank. 1⁵⁄₁₆", $250.00 – 350.00.

Democratic club, plain back, ⁵⁄₈", $20.00.

These buttons have cut steel pieces individually riveted to the button, ⁹⁄₁₆" to 1¹¹⁄₁₆".
Top row, left to right: Chased and tinted brass, $20.00. Buckle design, $12.00. Oval, $10.00.
Bottom row, left to right: Floral-like design, $18.00. Crescent and star, $7.00. Stamped brass, $18.00.

Paperweights

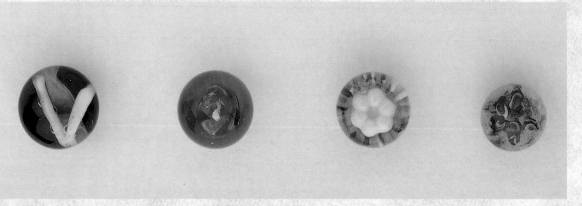

Winfield Rutter, *paperweight artist from the early 1940s to late 1950s. He made a variety of paperweight buttons, including stylistic flowers and roses, multicolored bases, cane swirls, and a few with an embedded floral-shaped glass bead. Although his floras are still collectible, they do not match the quality or detail of Kaziun or Ericson. In 1943, he made a red, white, and blue flag-like paperweight and the "V" for victory pictured above. His buttons are pear-shaped, and the base usually has different colored layers of glass visible from the side. The shanks on the above buttons include heavy round iron, copper, and brass shanks. $45.00; $20.00; $40.00; $25.00.*

Opposite page:

    Ray Banford and his wife Ruth have always admired antique glass. He became both a knowledgeable collector and dealer in old glass and antique desk weights. Ray's fascination led him and his son Robert to start experimenting with glass. Retiring in 1973, Ray started making mini desk weights and then evolved to full-size desk weights. By 1976, he was producing paperweight buttons. In both his early and later buttons, he used several types of shanks including copper, brass, and iron "U" shanks, and copper and brass loop shanks, both small eyed and large eyed. Per a phone conversation with Mr. Banford, he used what was available to him, which included wire from paperclips. He is best known for his Weymouth Rose and assorted florals, also pictured are millefiori cane setups. His caps include ball, dome, and pear-shaped. On the back of his paperweights is a small indentation, where he neatly pushed in the shank. Ray still makes desk weights on a limited basis, while his son Robert continues the tradition and is well-known in the field.

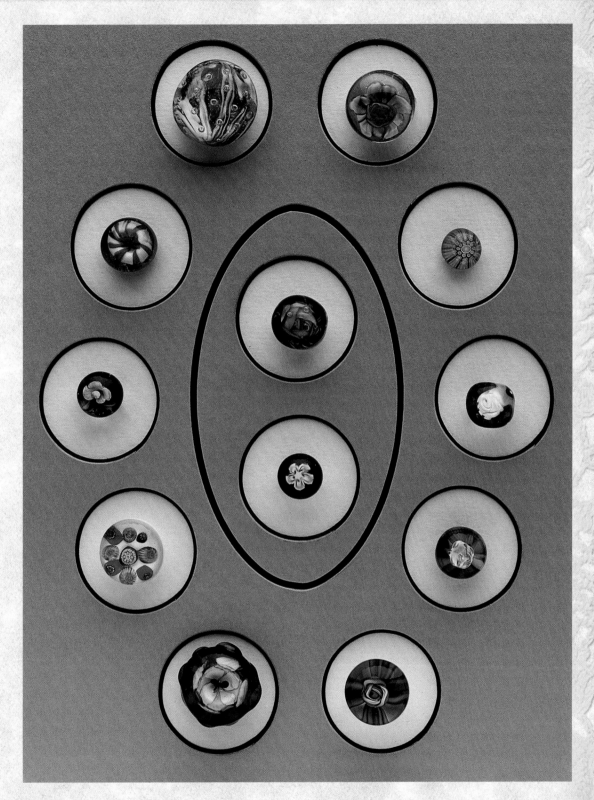

Ray Banford paperweight buttons, $25.00 – 75.00 for Weymouth Roses.

If you didn't know who he was, you'd never guess that this 6'5" soft-spoken, muscular man can finesse a torch with the best of them. **Robert Hansen** is the son of Ronald and Dorothy Hansen and was born and raised in Mackinaw City, Michigan. His parents were antique dealers and especially enjoyed old glass. His father was very talented and well known for his desk weights. His mother made paperweight buttons, but in a limited quantity. Ronald suffered from a stroke, so her attention was directed to taking care of her husband. Robert started making paperweight buttons when he was only 12 years old.

B.J. Smith and her husband Gordon were acquaintances of the family, through their mutual interest in desk weights. B.J. contacted Robert in 1982 to see if she could purchase some of his paperweight buttons, income which provided the young man extra money. In the 1980s he attended college to meet the necessary requirements for the civil service exam. He is now a prison guard in Upper Michigan. Robert's wife Lynn is very proud and supportive of her talented husband and always encourages him to pursue his career in glass.

Robert's father had amassed a large quantity of older French and Italian glass. Robert is still using his father's stock, so collectors can enjoy some magnificent colors unavailable to other glass artists. He also makes a few Christmas ornaments and desk weights. Ronald was very proud of his son's work and told him he would be a greater glass artist that he had been. Robert is proud not only to be known as Ronald's son but also as an accomplished glass artist in his own right.

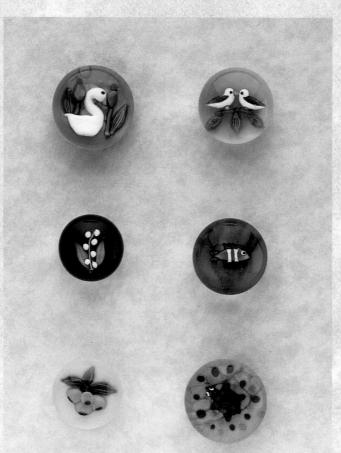

Swan: Blue base with goldstone cattails and multicolored striped leaves and stalks, $45.00.

Doves: Bright orange background and goldstone branch with multicolored striped leaves, $60.00.

Lily-of-the-valley: Black base, solid green leaves, and white flowers, $40.00.

Fish: Vibrant blue background with green goldstone weeds behind a tropical fish, $45.00.

Blueberries: True-to-life colored blueberries with multicolored leaves, $40.00.

Turtle: Sand-colored base with blue goldstone accents and the cutest little bug-eyed turtle, $45.00.

Buttons by Robert Hansen.

William Iorio made paperweight buttons from the late 1960s to 1970s. Pictured here is an original card of his paperweight buttons. In his glass shop in Flemington, New Jersey, he also produced desk weights and glass vases.

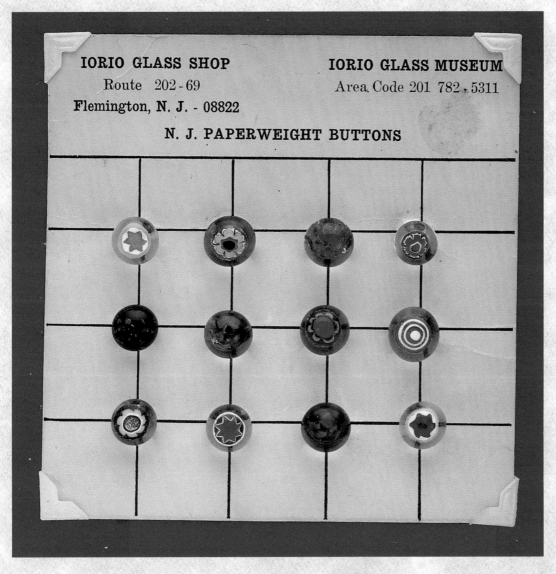

The shanks on these William Iorio buttons are heavy brass or steel and are deeply inserted, leaving a dimple-like area. $160.00 card.

Paperweights

So much has already been written about this long-time, very well-respected paperweight artists. **John Gooderham** is the type of person who always has a smile, makes one feel at ease, and is an all-around nice man.

John worked for 40 years in a steel plant as a millwright and now lives in Sault St. Marie, Ontario, Canada. He became very interested in glass after seeing an article on antique desk weights in a 1965 *Woman's Day* magazine. John later purchased two desk weights and was interested in how they might have been made. Shortly thereafter, he had a chance encounter with Ronald Hansen at a Detroit antique show. John was interested in learning how to make desk weights, but Hansen suggested he try making paperweight buttons. After several trips to Hansen's home, John acquired not only glass-working techniques, but a friend.

John started making paperweight buttons in 1976 and continues to do so. Collectors can find him at many state and national shows. While he has made a variety of glass items, including marbles, desk weights, and doll-house weights, he finds making buttons most enjoyable. John makes a variety of paperweight buttons, from foil-encased pictorials to flowers, and his specialty is millefiori. His latest endeavor involves his daughter, Jennine O'Connor. She is retired and does the hand painting for some of his paperweight buttons. Her skills as an artist and her enthusiasm for buttons are very much appreciated. John really enjoys the time that he gets to spend with Jennine while working on buttons together.

John has the initial "J" on all of his buttons, either on the back on in the set-up.

Facing page, clockwise from top right:

Large scramble: With lampwork cat, special year 2000 cane, made and signed by John, assorted full and partial millefiori with goldstone, $40.00.

Snow couple: This button is hand painted by Jennine O'Connor and enclosed and signed on the back by John. $60.00.

Mermaid: Also hand painted by Jennine. Mermaid, octopus, and tiny "J" cane, encased by John with his signature cane on the back, $40.00.

Country cabin scene: Another hand-painted scene by his daughter, encased by John with his signature cane on the back. $60.00.

Y2K: One of John's year 2000 paperweights, light blue base and goldstone, with his Y2K and "J" cane in the center, $35.00.

Floral: Beautiful blue-striped lampwork flower on a yellow background with a 24k gold foil bee floating above, $50.00.

2000: Blue and white millefiori canes surrounding John's 2000 and "J" cane, $35.00.

Rose: Long-stemmed 24k gold foil rose on deep blue background, floating above is a 24k gold bee, $40.00.

Patterned millefiori button, featuring canes from Pershire, Scotland, Italian mille, and complicated canes by John. $40.00.

Red: Three cut and faceted windows on side and one on top. White and red millefiori on pink base. $55.00.

Center: Basket: Double overlay yellow over white with a red flower and green leaves in center. The cutting on the basket is exclusive to Ed Poore of Cape Cod. $175.00.

John Gooderham paperweight buttons.

Nancy DuBois wanted to add glass lampworking to her skills as a button studio artist. In 1997 she took a local college course on the subject. She was quite frustrated with the technical side of this art and was unable to use what she had learned. She persuaded her husband Skip to take the course. Nancy knew he would be good at this type of artwork, as he has a natural understanding of the scientific side of glass. With Skip's patience and help, Nancy was able to achieve what she had wanted. In 2000, she started creating paperweight buttons. Her style is different than Skip's, and she leans toward a combination of charming and fun paperweights. Skip is a very detail-oriented paperweight artist, and appreciates a more traditional and classic style. Because of their differences, the glass studio is a harmonious and productive center for both of them. Collectors are lucky to have such a variety coming from both artists of the DuBois studio.

Facing page, clockwise from top:

Rose: White base with goldstone, green and orange glass, and clear cap. The rose pattern was impressed into the glass while still warm and filled with gold paint. Medium, $30.00.

Alarm clock: Back base with clear cap that enclosed tiny foil pieces that represent the digits. The alarm clock, clock hands, and clock feet are glass overlay. Medium, $35.00.

Peacock: Cobalt blue base with goldstone, finely etched silver foil feathers enclosed by a clear glass cap. The peacock's body and face are glass overlay. Medium, $75.00.

Gingerbread man: Amber-colored base with goldstone, clear and white glass overlay for eyes, nose, and buttons. Medium, $35.00.

Bird: Transparent light green base with goldstone and millefiori cane. Uplifted wings and tail and overlay black glass eyes. Large, $35.00.

Purse: Pink base with clear cap that encloses tiny silver foil coins. The purse closure and handle are glass overlay on the cap. She embedded tiny rhinestones while the glass was still warm. Medium, $35.00.

Center, top to bottom:

Moon face and star: Cobalt blue base with goldstone, clear cap enclosing etched silver foil moon face and star. Medium, $30.00.

Hot air balloon: White base with a thin layer of blue glass and a transparent cap that encloses a finely detailed etched silver foil hot air balloon. The clouds are a very thin overlay of white glass. Medium, $40.00.

Nancy DuBois paperweight buttons.

Paperweights

Skip DuBois farms and resides in New Jersey with his wife Nancy and children. He is also an accomplished dulcimer player. Skip became interested in buttons after meeting his wife and soon found that he was attached to the glass ones. He enrolled in classes in advanced art glass and found it very rewarding and challenging. With a lot of encouragement and help from friend and glassworker John Gooderham, Skip turned his attention to making his own unique style of paperweight buttons. His production is very limited, as much time is spent exploring new techniques. Innovative in his work, he has introduced several firsts to paperweight buttons. Among them are the stave basket, full botanicals, bouquets, lace grounds, realistics, and accurately scaled crown weights. He is very precise about the shape of his caps and the layout of his canes. He pays special attention to the subject presented in his paperweights, making sure they are correctly centered. His backs are very clean and neat and easy to mount. His floral paperweights rival any on the market and resemble the work of the late paperweight artist Thure Ericson. I am very pleased to be the first to present his work in book form.

Facing page, clockwise from top right:

Gumball machine: The first realistic shaped paperweight. White-based globe that holds millefiori candies, $35.00+.

Floral: Shaded apricot-colored petals, yellow stamen, and recurved leaves that rest on a cushion of white lace, $50.00+.

Pear: Blushed pear with vein-shaded leaf and blossom end at bottom for added realism, $45.00+.

Millefiori: Cobalt blue base with millefiori canes, laid on in a spoke design alternating between green and white with a daisy in the center, $25.00+.

Floral: Upright flower, fully dimensional, variegated and recurved leaves. Petals surround a complex 24-piece stamen. This all floats above a cushion of white lace, $55.00+.

Rabbit in stave basket: Millefiori radiates from the bottom of the button and curves upward to form a basket for the rabbit. Skip has done limited numbers of this button because of the difficulty of this process. Stave basket is borrowed from old French and English desk paperweight makers. $65.00+.

Floral: This dimensional flower rests on a goldstone and transparent dark green base. $45.00+.

Moon and stars: Millefiori canes of white stars surrounding a yellow moon set on a cobalt blue base. $25.00+.

Floral: Morning glory blossom shading from blue to white with dainty orange and yellow stamen, floating above a transparent cranberry base. $45.00+.

Fishbowl: A blue fish swims past wispy seaweed. Skip placed three air bubbles coming from the fish's mouth. This is the second realistic paperweight button. $60.00+.

Center, top to bottom:

Crown: Twisted filigree and alternating twisted ribbon wrap to meet a multi-petaled flower with stamen at the top of this paperweight. This miniature is true to scale to full-size paperweights that were popular in Victorian times. It is an exceptional button viewed from the side and unique to Skip. $85.00+.

Botanical: Entire plant from blossoms to roots. Each plant takes several hours to complete before the button can be started. Glass artists have done botanicals for years, but never before in buttons. This is the type of attention to detail and craftsmanship that Skip has mastered. $85.00+.

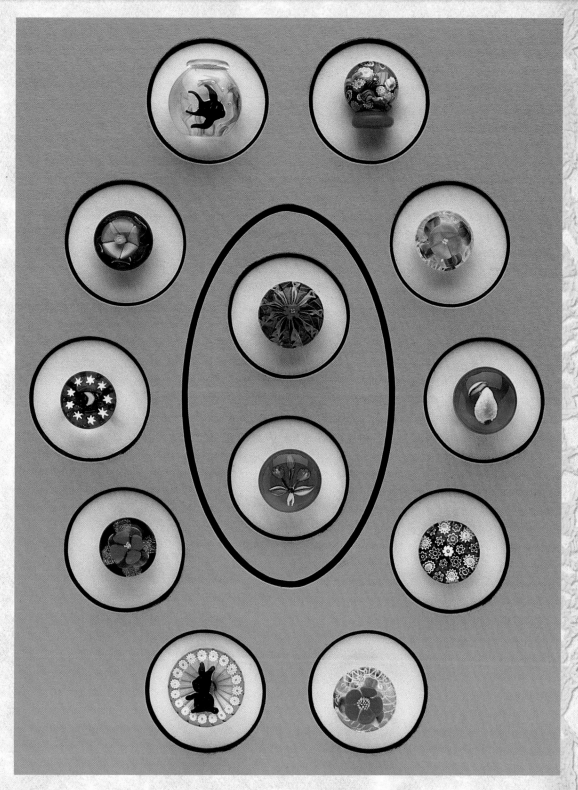

Skip DuBois paperweight buttons.

Paperweights

Sue Fox began working with glass after attending a bead symposium in 1994. Her love of glass, along with the desire to work on a very small scale, led her to focus on paperweight buttons. Sue's work includes a variety of subjects inspired by nature, such as dragonflies, bumblebees, and birds with nests. A signature cane is used on most of her paperweights. It is a cross between an S and an F, on white with a blue edge. Some of her buttons have Fox and the year etched on the back. She has won awards at the Embellishment Show in 1998 and Bead and Button Show in 2000. Sue grew up in Spartanburg, South Carolina, and now resides in Columbia, South Carolina, where she works from her home studio.

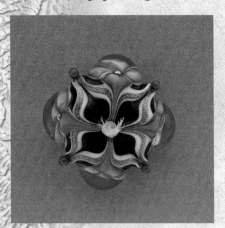

A less traditional button, the Floral Square has encased flowers with an incised central design. Medium, $65.00 – 75.00.

Dinah Hulet is half of a sister-run company called Hulet Glass in northern California. Presently her time is spent concentrating on making facial canes. She designs and makes all of her own canes, which may take her from several hours to several days. She has taught classes on this labor-intensive technique at the Corning Museum of Glass and Penland School of Crafts. Dinah is also considered an expert in bead and marble making but does this now only for special exhibitions. An embellishment show in the mid-1990s was her first display of her paperweight buttons. Dinah's wide range of projects and busy schedule allow her to make buttons only on special request. Most of her paperweight buttons are signed "Hulet" and dated.

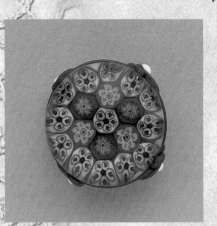

I like this button because of the glass overlay bands and added decoration on the outside of the cap. The center is millefiori, and the back is signed "hulet/96." Medium, $55.00 – 65.00.

Charles Kaziun *produced paperweight buttons from the 1940s – 1950s. This is an example of his "bubble" paperweights. His florals, foil cut outs, and silhouettes are highly prized by collectors and command a much higher price than the one pictured here. The name Kaziun is widely known for the quality desk weights he produced. $50.00.*

William C. Stokes was born in Maryland in 1954. His neighborhood was next to a forest, which he spent many hours exploring. Will was always studying birds and bringing home frogs and snakes, much to his mother's dismay. His wintertime projects were drawing animals and building ships inside bottles.

After high school, Will moved to northern California and lived in the woods to get away from the troubled times of the 1970s. He spent his time enjoying nature and playing the bagpipes. In the early 1980s, Will moved to the eastern part of Washington state and lived in a cabin in a semi-remote area, making willow baskets and furniture from basket willow he had grown. In 1988, he moved to Bellingham and had his first chance at blowing glass. There was a torch available in the studio, and he started experimenting with glass by making beads and small glass animals. This is where he met his future wife Julie Clinton, and they started working with glass together.

Julie was born in Wenatchee, Washington, in 1958. She lived on the outskirts of town and spent many happy hours hiking and playing in the hills and observing plants and animals. After graduating from high school, she went on to study plants and obtained a degree in botany. After college, she spent several years working for the Forest Service and Department of Natural Resources. Her jobs were varied and included trail building, fire suppression, helicopter logging, tree planting, etc. She moved to Bellingham in 1987, where she lived with some glass blowers. Julie met Will while taking a wilderness first aid class. They began their business in 1989, naming it Blue Flame Studios and sold their beads and goblets at small arts and crafts shows in the Pacific Northwest area.

William Blanning introduced Will and Julie to the world of button collecting. They were attending a bead conference when he complimented them on their work. The following day he brought his precious collection of paperweight buttons with him to the show. Blanning said, "With your talent, you should be making paperweight buttons." How lucky for button collectors that they listened to him.

They initially made the paperweights with the usual hand and torch technique for the base, set-up and cap. Many of their paperweights are now made with what is called "vacuum encasement." There is only a slight difference between their old and new methods. The vacuum method is done by melting and dripping hot glass into a vacuum chamber, which pulls the glass down and around the set-up. Next they fire polish and shape the cap and add their signature canes and copper shank to the base. The final button is placed in the kiln to anneal for 30 minutes at 960° Fahrenheit.

Button collectors keep them very busy with requests for certain themes for their trays. Julie and Will use this inspiration in their work and continue to enjoy the challenge. Most of their buttons have their signature cane "WS" or "JC," except for the silver line and the mosaic canes, which by their uniqueness are attributed to them. They do not sign their diminutives due to lack of space.

Will has taught lampworking classes with Paul Stankard at the Pilchuck Glass School, Washington, and the Studio of Corning Glass in Corning, New York. Will and Julie have also taught in New Zealand, Canada, and various places throughout the United States.

Will and Julie live on five acres in Whatcom County, Washington, where they cleared the land and built their own home and studio. Living in the woods has many advantages, and they incorporate their surroundings in their work.

Owl with silver foil, signature cane
WS 97, $75.00.

Old paperweight buttons with swirlbacks, thin wire loop shanks, $12.00 – 18.00.

Thure Ericson *made beautiful floral paperweights from the early 1940s to early 1960s. Of all the paperweights artists from that time period, his florals are my favorite. Many of his flowers start at the base and spring upward, while others float above the base. The backs of his buttons are smooth with a small indentation where he inserted his shanks. all three buttons pictured have a thin, flat, iron wire shank. Top, $80.00. Bottom left, $90.00. Bottom right, $60.00.*

Paperweight artist **Ken Shay** is very comfortable with details. His job as a dentist with the Department of Veterans Affairs in Ann Arbor, Michigan, provides him the patience for working with small objects. As a form of relaxation, he attended a bead making class. Upon seeing his beads, an old friend mentioned how they looked like paperweight buttons. In late 1997, he made his first buttons. In the spring of 1998, he took a class at Corning Glass in New York to guide him in creating his own canes. Ken also does marbles and desk paperweights. To date he has made between 300 and 400 paperweight buttons. He uses latticinio canes, dichroic glass, and his own pictorial canes. All of his buttons are signed and dated.

Examples of Ken Shay paperweight buttons,
$30.00 – 40.00.

Theresa Rarig started making sulphide paperweight buttons in the early 1960s. She molded and fired the paperweights in a kiln, and after cooling, a gold-colored metal shank and plate were glued on. The tops are slightly rounded and the glass is very thick, some look like miniature cupcakes. Before paperweights, she made ceramic and assorted glass buttons.

Elephant head, 1¼", $35.00. Former President Jimmy Carter,
$25.00. Jenny Lind, $20.00. Teddy Bear, $20.00.

Elaine LaFlex-Green *is a bead artist who start-ed making paperweight buttons in 1998. Her early ones were unsigned while others were etched "EP" or "P". Elaine's latest buttons have signature "P" or "L-G" canes. Designs include florals, teddy bears, fruits, spiders, and aquarium scenes, $15.00.*

Allison Lindquist, *self shank, marked 96. Small, $10.00.*

Jacque Israel *made paperweight buttons from the early 1940s to 1960s. His paperweights are easy to identify due to their mechanical makeup. The backs of his buttons are very rough and uneven. The buttons pictured have either a large iron "U" shank or smaller metal loop shank. The top row center button is twisted ribbon overlay over clear glass. The bottom center button is an example of his sulphide; the rest are ribbon canes with rounded domes, $30.00 – 40.00.*

Plastics

The British Artid Plastics Company started in February of 1939 in Slough, Berkshire, England, just before WWII. Two German brothers, Manfred and Rudolph Bamburger, owned the company. In 1940 the factory was producing plastic mounts for cameras which were mounted on fighter aircraft. At the end of the war, the factory started making cameos, prayer book covers, cigarette boxes, perfume bottles, and other utilitarian products for top international companies.

In 1946, they started making buttons. All are back marked "Artid, Made in England." They are compression molded and classified as Thermoset plastics. The buttons were not a commercial success and one year later they stopped making them. Because of the limited time they were made, some of the designs are considered scarce.

Large quantities of the buttons were found in a World War II air raid shelter several years ago and purchased by Jim and Rita Stephenson. Many of the buttons are being sold to clothing designers. One famous designer purchased some for his spring collection. They are also being purchased by non-button collectors who also collect other items that the company made.

Courtesy of Jim and Rita Stephenson's website article.

Artid buttons. Large, 1½", $10.00 – 15.00.

Artid buttons.
Medium, 1", $6.00 – 8.00.

Artid buttons.
Medium, 1" to 1 ¼", $6.00 – 10.00.

Many collectors have embraced these modern plastic buttons we call "snap-togethers." I was first attracted to them in the mid-1990s, although they have been around since the 1980s. The top of the button, which has the shank, is snapped into the bottom piece, which is another color. This type of construction is called "shank involvement." On some, the backside of the button has the shank, and the top piece is attached in another manner; this style is called "no shank involvement." Most, but not all, have been imported from countries like Japan, England, and France. Tom and Jerry and moveable balls, $4.00 – 6.00. Others, $1.00 – 2.00 each.

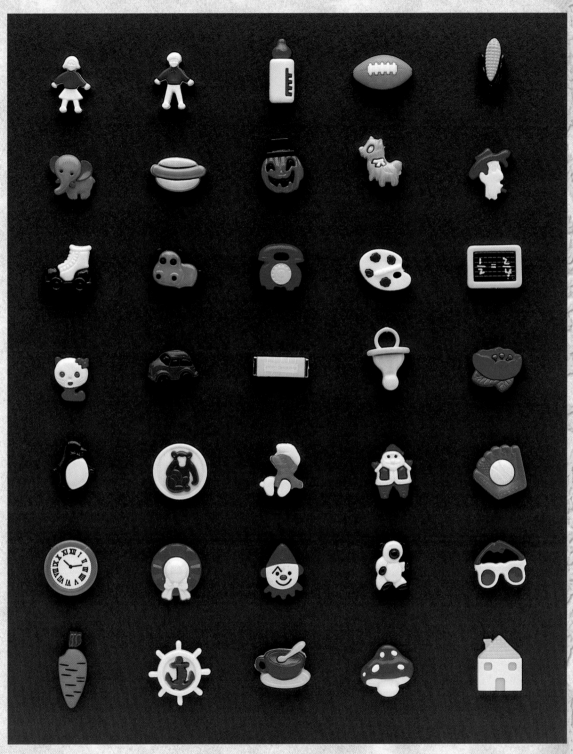

Snap-togethers, $1.00 – 2.00, Smurf, $3.00.

Lucite is the trade name for the chemical methyl methacrylate which was discovered by the DuPont Company in 1931. During WWII it was used for making windshields and various components on fighter planes, then in the late 1940s through the 1950s it was used for combs and numerous jewelry pieces. The above buttons range in size from ¾" to 1½".

Row 1: $5.00, $12.00, $10.00.
Row 2: $12.00, $12.00.
Row 3: $10.00, $3.00, $6.00.
Row 4: $8.00, $6.00.
Row 5: $25.00, $15.00, $15.00.

*Clear and colored plastic
combination. Large, $8.00.*

*Dried flowers encased in
plastic. Medium, $7.00.*

*Gold painted plastic buttons with a string of glass beads glued in a
circular pattern. $5.00 – 8.00.*

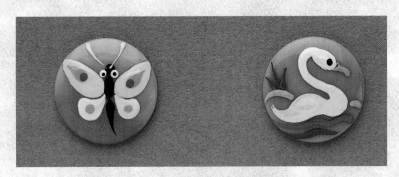

*Two examples of hand-painted plastic buttons done by Edith and Alan J. Brooks in the 1960s.
Together, this husband and wife team from England created a very distinctive painting style. Subjects
included, but were not limited to, frogs, insects, birds, people, fish, golliwogs, Christmas themes,
miscellaneous animals, and an assortment of florals. This couple hand painted hundreds of buttons,
but they were never mass-produced. Brooks buttons have gone up considerably in the past few years.
Butterfly and swan, $^{11}/_{16}$", $35.00 – 40.00 each.*

Both of these very large thermoplastic buttons are imitation tortoise shell.
Left, $8.00. Right, metal-embellished, $10.00.

    The National Button Society has recently revised the entire 9-A plastics section called Synthetic Polymers. Thermoset and thermoplastic types of buttons are separately classed and described. Thermosets include Bakelite and Catalin, and thermoplastics include Lucite, Fimo, and Rhodoid. The recent publication of two books on plastic buttons will be helpful to both the novice and advanced collector.

Left: Black glass beads embedded in black plastic, backmarked
"22 Carasso 22 Milan," $6.00.
Right: Black glass beaded center surrounded by iridescent sequins
on black plastic, backmarked "14 Expedit 14 aris" on shank plate,
circa 1950s, $8.00.

Noh Masks are used in Japanese dance-drama. Arita Porcelain.
Medium, $35.00 – 45.00 each.

Six nations, painted glass ladies' heads, circa 1940s. Hungarian, Spanish, Turkish,
Scotch, Dutch, and French. $30.00 – 40.00 set.

Flag set, heavy gilt brass and enamel, long brazed-on shank, circa 1940s.
$65.00 – 75.00 set.
Top row: USA, Great Britain, France, Mexico, Ireland, and Sweden.
Bottom row: Chile, Italy, Czechoslovakia (Czech Republic), Brazil, Cuba, and Argentina.

Pearl realistics, $4.00 – 8.00 set.

French realistics, plastic,
$2.00 – 3.00 each.

"Dice" set, plastic, $17.00 set.

Bakelite flowers, 1 ¹⁵/₁₆", $30.00 each.

The Mah Jongg Winds set, celluloid, $20.00 set.

This is one of my favorite Bakelite realistics. This large 1 ³/₄" x 2 ⁷/₁₆" anchor has a working compass. $75.00.

Baby chick sitting in eggshell, made of "casein," a thermoset plastic, $6.00.

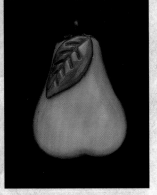

$12.00.

$5.00.

$7.00.

$10.00.

*These buttons are hollow
two-piece celluloids.*

$12.00.

$15.00.

$15.00.

Luggage, celluloid, $15.00 – 18.00 each.

*Coffee pot and creamer, celluloid,
$8.00 – 12.00 each.*

*Old Southwest, complete set consists of steer, tepee, Indian head, bison,
vaquero head and horse head (missing from photo). They are made of heavy
brass with a large attached brass shank. $40.00 – 50.00 set.*

*These ceramic animals have a transparent blue glaze, gold paint, and a tiny embedded wire
shank. It is obvious that they belong together, but I do not know who made them or if this is
a complete representation, circa 1940s, $5.00 – 8.00 each.*

Bakelite numbers. NBS large,
$8.00 – 10.00 each.

Celluloid fruits with large center rhinestone. Flat backs with attached celluloid
shank, partial set. NBS small,
$8.00 each.

Mexican Set, possibly incomplete, white plastic, hard to find.
Medium, $6.00 – 8.00 each.

Marion Weber was an accomplished designer for B. Blumenthal & Co. She began designing buttons for their LaMode® line in the late 1930s. Her celluloid seed packets, candies, pastries, candles, and fruit buttons were a refreshing change for the dress trade. During the 1940s and 1950s, she also designed sets like the metalized plastic Dress Makers Set and the solid metal Detective and Busy Bee sets. Even at that time, they were considered deluxe buttons and were very costly. Weber designs are highly sought after by today's collectors for their overall charm and workmanship. All of the below buttons are made of celluloid, which makes them very susceptible to deterioration.

Fruit crop, a nine-piece set of oranges, bananas, cherries, grapes, peaches, strawberries, mixed fruit, pears, and apples. $20.00 – 25.00 each.

These two buttons are part of the eight Birdlings pictured in the September 1958 issue of the National Button Society newsletter. I could find no reference about whether or not the woodpecker, cardinal, robin, wren, sparrow, bluebird, bird with orange breast, and a brown and gray bird were considered a complete set. $20.00 each.

Crated fruit, an eight-button set, apples (pictured), oranges, strawberries, pears, mixed fruits, bananas, peaches, and blueberries. $20.00 – 25.00 each.

Bakelite flower with red painted center, metal loop shank. Large, $25.00.

Leather guitar. Large, $8.00 – 12.00.

Match sticks, heavy painted metal with loop shank, $8.00 – 12.00.

Plastic bow, large, sew-thru, $6.00.

Umbrella, celluloid, hard to find.
Large, $25.00.

Baseball, celluloid, attached cellu-
loid shank. Large, $10.00.

Pumpkin with hat and metal loop
shank. Medium, $10.00.

Swan, made of casein with
metal loop shank.
Medium, $15.00.

Rabbit. Large, $6.00.

Tomato half, celluloid,
$10.00 – 15.00.

163

Bakelite realistics.

From top left: Star, $8.00; heart w/arrow, $12.00; bow, $6.00; spaniel, $10.00; hand w/metal bracelet, $12.00; dagger, $15.00; face, $25.00; spaceman, $18.00; rabbit, $12.00; riding boot, $22.00; anchor, $15.00; mailbox, $25.00; leaf, $18.00.

Pirate's face, hand carved with painted detail and a chain earring. Large, $15.00 – 20.00.

Three wooden hats: Green hat has a thin wire staple shank. The red and blue ones have heavy brass loop shanks and are made of a better quality wood. Green, $4.00; red, $8.00; blue, $8.00.

This is one of my favorite wood buttons. I am still amazed at the time and workmanship put into some of the vintage realistics. This large concave basket holds a carrot, pea, and onion. Each vegetable is held in place by a tiny screw on the backside, and button has a brass loop shank. Stamped into the back is CZECHO - SLOVAKIA. Large, 1⅛" x 1¾". $15.00 – 18.00.

Cute as a button are these two wooden suitcases. Both have a metal loop shank. The green suitcase has stamped into the back B.G.E. Orig. Yellow, $10.00. Green, $15.00.

Teenage Mutant Ninja Turtles were very popular cartoon characters from a 1984 comic book. By 1988, parents were rushing to the stores to hunt for action figures, videos, trading cards, and numerous Ninja Turtle items. Streamline Industries produced these buttons for a limited time, and in 1998 the company was purchased by Blumenthal Lansing. Buttons came in both medium and large sizes. Left to right: Raphael, Donatello, Leonardo, and Michelangelo, early 1990s. Large, $8.00 each.

Disney buttons from Australia, circa 1940s.
Row 1: Donald Duck, painted metal, $6.00 – 8.00.
Row 2: Pluto, plastic, $8.00 – 10.00.
Row 3: Chip and Bambi, plastic, $8.00 – 10.00.

These wonderful china head doll buttons were available in this 1953 catalog from the Mark Farmer Manufacturing. Co. for $1.00 each. The company, from El Cerrito, California, started in 1946 making utilitarian pottery items. A few years later, they were producing individual china doll heads, legs, and arms, and complete dressed dolls named Jennie June and James. Through a phone conversation with Mr. Farmer, I learned that he had made a mold from one of his mother's vintage dolls. This mold and others to follow were used to make all the Jennie June items which were cast, hand-painted, and fired by his employees. A half-face mold was used to make the buttons. The catalog also includes Jennie June lamp bases, cookie jars, salt and pepper shakers, and wall plaques. They were made for a limited time, as later catalogs do not feature them.

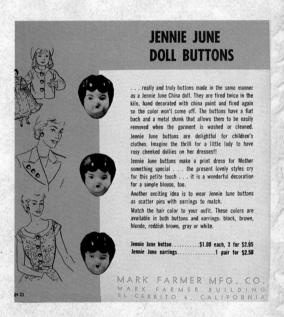

There were six hair colors available. Pictured are black, blonde, reddish brown, and brown.
Not shown are gray and white. Heavy, embedded brass wire loop shank, circa early 1950s.
$25.00 – 35.00 each.

Tony the Tiger, Snap, Crackle, and Pop, Cornelius, Coco, Sunny, and Toucan Sam are familiar Kellogg's™ cereal characters that are sure to be future collectibles. The two sets pictured include eight hand-painted metal and five hand-painted wood buttons. Manufactured for JHB International in 1998, they were sold by button dealers, sewing shops, and the Kellogg's Store in Battle Creek, Michigan. They are no longer being made. $3.00 – 5.00 each.

Hand painted porcelain fruit, vegetable, and dessert buttons from Thailand.
Purchased from button dealer Annie Fraser in 1998.
All are either medium or large and have a glued-on clear plastic shank.
$3.00 each at time of purchase.

More hand–painted porcelain buttons from Thailand. $3.00 each at time of purchase.

Bakelite playing card symbols, small (missing diamond from set), 1940s, $5.00 each, $25.00 complete set.

Painted plastic purse, circa 1940s. Large, $10.00 – 12.00.

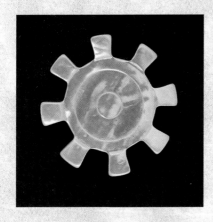

Pearl ship's wheel, inserted two-hole metal shank, circa 1940s. Medium, $8.00.

This hand-carved turquoise bear and several others were purchased by button maker/designer Paco Despachio in the late 1980s. The man he bought them from stated they were from China but did not know how old they were. In the late 1990s, Paco drilled a hole and added a brass shank. NBS large studio button, $25.00.

Vintage plastic, Bakelite, and celluloid realistics.
Cigarette pack, $15.00 – 18.00. All others, $3.00 – 6.00 each.

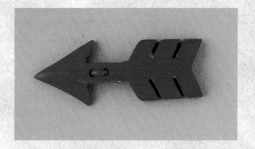

Casein arrow, 1⅞", $6.00.

*Celluloid
matchstick.
Large, $12.00.*

*Hand painted bone button. Just unscrew the
shank and roll the dice! $25.00.*

*Main characters of the popular TV show, "The Simpsons." Lampword glass buttons from
the Czech Republic, set purchased in 1999 for $25.00. I expect these to rise in value as
time passes. Left to right: Marge, Maggie, Lisa, Bart, and Homer.*

Glass fruits with four-way box shank. $6.00 – 8.00 each.

Vintage Bakelite. Die, $5.00; hat, $10.00; die, $6.00; fish, $6.00; dog face, $7.00.

Bakelite tulip. Large, $20.00.

Bakelite, $7.00 – 10.00 each.

Colorful modern metal buttons with cold plastic enamel, a liquid that hardens without heat, circa 1990s, $5.00 – 8.00 each.

Heavy metal dog buttons, designed by Todd Old–ham. Not pictured are the matching dog bones. Sold in the early 1990s. $8.00 – 10.00 each.

Vintage wood realistics.

Horseshoe, $7.00; shoe, $3.00; old woman's face, $10.00; shoe sole, $3.00; leaf, $8.00; apple, $6.00; acorn, $5.00; elephant head, $12.00.

Russian

The Russian papier-maché buttons are some of the most beautifully detailed hand-painted buttons available to collectors. Although the buttons are new, they have Old World charm. There are generally only three buttons made in each design. Most of the artists live near Moscow, and some of them are farmers that paint at night. The button blank is made by one artist and hand painted by another. Several coats of lacquer are applied over the oil-painted image, giving it a brilliant shine. This method is the same they have been using for over 200 years. Each button has a self-shank, an artist signature, and subject title hand painted on the back. All have a gold border either in a line design or decorative pattern. Average size is 1¼" to 1½". The Russians are very accomplished artists, and there is no limit to the wide variety of animals, people, structures, and scenes to choose from. These are not studio buttons, but considered modern, as they have been sold commercially.

Facing page, from left, top to bottom:

African lion, $48.00.
Winter scene, with pearl inlay sky, $57.00.
Great spangled fritillary (butterfly), $48.00.
Kate Greenaway summer, $48.00.

Little Sable lighthouse, $48.00.
Peacock, $48.00.
Ice skaters with scene in background, $48.00.
Hungry wolf, $48.00.

Lady bugs, reproduced in the Fabergé style. Enamel over a guilloche ground and embellished with Austrian crystals. Made in St. Petersburg, Russia and purchased in 1998. There are other Fabergé-style enamel items, like spoons, pendants, and brooches on the market, although buttons seem to be more elusive, $75.00.

Russian papier-maché angel, hand painted and signed "M.H. 1995," $12.00.

Facing page:

These are more examples of the delicate work done by today's Russian artists, large hand painted pearl oval discs, mounted in German silver with twisted rope borders. The photograph does not capture the fine detail in these works of art that measure 2$\frac{1}{16}$" x 1$\frac{1}{2}$". Each button is artist signed, dated, and covered with a clear finish to protect the paint. Shown are various women's heads, but I have also seen Russian scenes and animals. They are considered modern and not studio buttons, dated 1997 and 1998. $50.00 – 60.00 each.

Shell

Assorted iridescent and non-iridescent shell buttons, types consist of ocean pearls, green snail, tiger cowrie, and abalone. Medium to large, $4.00 – 10.00 each.

Assorted shell buttons, ¾" to 1¼".
Vertical rows from left, top to bottom:

Carved floral design, four-way metal shank, $18.00. Engraved building scene, sew-thru,
$30.00. Engraved stylistic bird, sew-thru, $20.00.
Pierced and gilded pearl, with floral pin shank, $20.00. Pierced, engraved and gold-filled lines,
sew-thru, $12.00. Carved pearl with gold paint-filled lines, pearlized center and swagged
brass shank, $8.00.
Engraved initial "B", drilled brass shank, swagged, $30.00. Gold-filled engraved lines, on
green snail, sew-thru, $15.00. Engraved fan, gold-filled lines, green snail, sew-thru, $25.00.

Colorful iridescent pearl button with eight
cut steels and white pearl center insert. 1 ¾".
$15.00 – 20.00.

Unusual pearls, chased metal insert held
in place by three cut steel rivets. 1 ⁹/₁₆".
$15.00 – 20.00.

1 ⁷/₁₆" pearl with metal anchor and rope
held in place by two steel rivets.
Large, $20.00.

Carved cameo pearl, prong set in
brass, with 26 large cut steels
around the border. 1 ⁷/₁₆".
$100.00 – 125.00.

Assorted shell buttons, first four are small, last one is medium. Left to right: Insect, $12.00. Bird on trellis, $16.00. Fabulous dragon, $12.00. Oriental man, $12.00. Four Oriental figures, $20.00 – 25.00.

More beautiful shell buttons. Small, $3.00 – 6.00 each.

Assorted shell buttons with metal embellishment. Openwork metal, megaphone, fan, basket, stars, floral, doorknocker. All NBS small, $6.00 – 10.00 each.

Carved oval pearl, 1 ³/₁₆" x 1⁷/₁₆", $10.00.

Small pearl button with enamel floral escutcheon and cut steels. $12.00 – 15.00.

1 ⅛", carved pearl, $15.00 – 18.00.

Pierced pearl. Large, $12.00.

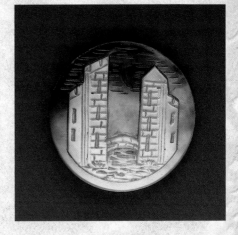

*Thick pearl, carved in a rose
design and held in place by
two pins to a flat pearl disc.
1¹⁄₁₆", sew-thru,
$40.00 – 50.00.*

*Fabulous cameo carved castle scene,
odd four-way metal shank, 1⁷⁄₁₆",
$100.00 – 125.00.*

*Dark gray pearl with inlaid
abalone shell, swagged in brass
shank, 1½", $12.00.*

Carved pearl. Large, $15.00.

*Cameo carved shell buttons, prong set with cut steel borders.
Left to right: Woman by house, $40.00. Horse head, $25.00. Woman, $20.00.
Rose, $35.00. Bust, $30.00.*

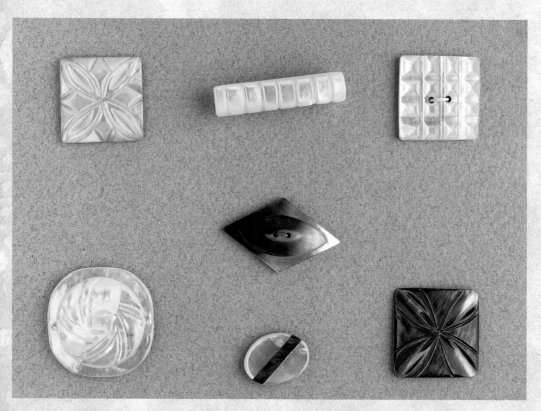

Shell, various shapes. Medium to large, $4.00 – 7.00 each.

Carved and pierced Jordan Pearls from Bethlehem, circa 1940s to 1950s. Rooster, large, $40.00. Cross, large, $35.00.

Three charming buttons by studio artist Nancy DuBois.

Kate Greenaway Twinklby Twins, hand-etched and pigmented, on a heart-shaped conch shell. Large, $45.00.
Cat, cameo carved cat scratching at the moon on dark iridescent pearl, silver stars for embellishment. Large, $45.00.
Windmill scene, etched and pigmented on a mother-of-pearl button, another fine example of Nancy's quality work and attention to detail. Large, $45.00.

Two more by Nancy DuBois. Basket, hand-carved cowrie shell,
with basket pattern at bottom and carved flowers near the top.
Nancy added garnet beads on silver wire
for grapes. $60.00.
Sunflower, hand-carved cowrie shell, $22.00.

These large pen or pinna shells have been fine line engraved by hand, then pigmented in gold. They have a metal loop shank that is set into the shell. Some of the designs on this type of shell will include jewels and metals for embellishments, as well as carving and piercing. Nancy numbers most of her buttons, except for what she calls her fun buttons. Her numbering system goes like this: example 010327 means that it was made in January (01), the next (0) means nothing until she has made over 1,000 buttons, (327) means it was the 327th button that she made in that particular type of material. The year is generally marked somewhere else on the back of the button.

Lady golfer with seed opal for golf ball. Signed ND, 1997, numbered
010327, marked 3 of 10. $55.00.
Swallow with three children, signed ND, 2001, numbered 030701,
marked 1 of 1, To Deb W. $50.00.
Orchid with Swarovksi stones in center. Signed ND, 1997, numbered
010338. $55.00.
All three buttons are by Nancy DuBois.

Original store cards.
Fashionable Buttons by LaMode, showing a variety of color choices. $12.00 − 15.00 per card.

*Clockwise from top left: Blue glass hats, $10.00. Plastic Canasta set, $15.00.
Purple transparent glass bows, $12.00. Yellow glass moonglows, $15.00.*

Costumakers
TRADE MARK

Finest Quality Imported

10¢

Pattern 6125 – Size 24''' – 3 on card

green

GUARANTEED WASHABLE

Made in Western Germany

Costumakers
TRADE MARK

Finest Quality Imported

10¢

Pattern 6137 – Size 30'' – 2 on card (S 8)

red

GUARANTEED WASHABLE

MADE IN WESTERN GERMANY

Costumakers
TRADE MARK

10¢

Pattern 6140 - size 30" - 2 on card

PINK

GUARANTEED WASHABLE

Western-Germany

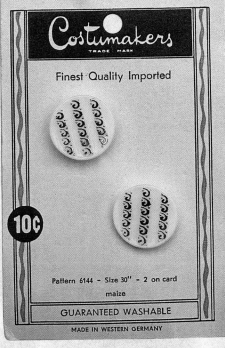

Costumakers
TRADE MARK

Finest Quality Imported

10¢

Pattern 6144 - Size 30'' - 2 on card

maize

GUARANTEED WASHABLE

MADE IN WESTERN GERMANY

Costumakers
TRADE MARK

Finest Imported Quality

10¢

Pattern 6134 - size 24" - 3 on card

LT. BLUE

GUARANTEED WASHABLE

Western-Germany

Group of assorted glass buttons on original Costumakers cards. $5.00 – 7.00 per card.

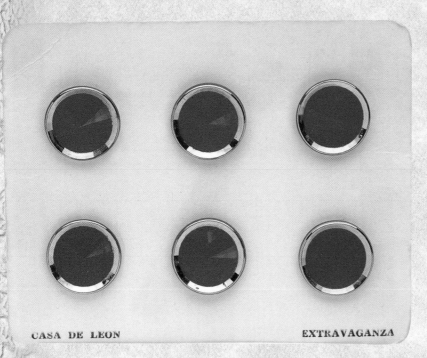

CASA DE LEON   EXTRAVAGANZA

Vintage red glass with silver luster. Medium, $15.00 card.

No. 5079—25—(5/8")—3 on—GREEN

Germany - US - Zone

Le Chic cards, clockwise from top: Green moonglows on a card marked moonstone, $10.00. Floral, $8.00. Hearts, $10.00.

25¢

4 buttons on card   GREEN
PATTERN 5010-SIZE 30-(5/8 INCH)

Made in Germany · US-Zone

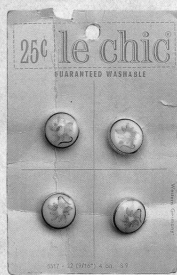

25¢ le chic
GUARANTEED WASHABLE

5517 - 22 (9/16") 4 on $9

Coconut shell buttons and buckle on a decorative original card. $30.00 – 40.00.

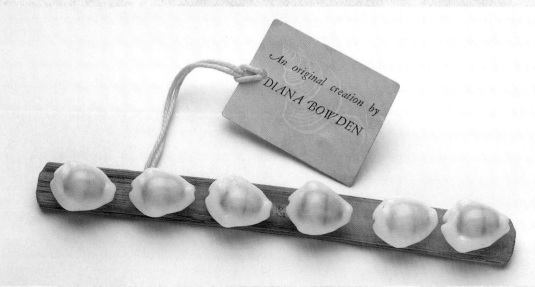

Real shell buttons on original wood mounting with attached paper label. Cemented-on brass loop shank and plate, $20.00 – 25.00 set.

"The Cisco Kid" was a popular radio show in the 1940s, which became a television series that ran from 1950 to 1956. $15.00.

Glass fruit set, $15.00.

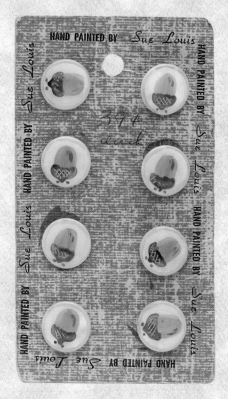

Hand-painted acorns by Sue Louis on small size pearls, $15.00 card.

Buttons by Schwanda.
Fruit, $8.00. Birds, $10.00. All others, $4.00 – 7.00 per card.

Yellow glass with gold luster.
Small, $10.00 – 15.00.

Blue glass with gold luster.
Small, $10.00 – 15.00.

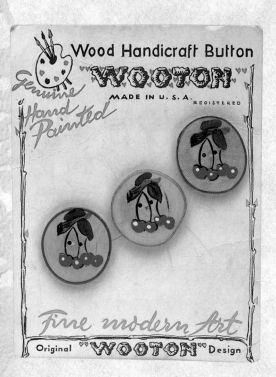

Cherries, hand painted on wood slices. On the
back of the card is stamped 25¢, 1950s.
Medium, $18.00 – 20.00.

The First Moon Landing, lightweight, metal,
circa 1969, $7.00 each.

Buttons by **Stella Rzanski.**

Satsuma-like, $15.00 and $12.00;
jasperware, $10.00 and $7.00.

Shirley Shaw, already a button collector, started making plastics buttons from liquid resin in the late 1960s. At the same time, she also made some decoupage on wood and a few simple ceramic buttons. Most of her early buttons are not signed. In the early 1970s, she and her sister Stella took ceramic classes. Both ladies took examples of their buttons to club members, and soon everyone wanted the lovely porcelain buttons called jasperware. They make their own molds either from replicas of old buttons or designs found on jewelry. Making the jasperware buttons is a time-consuming process which takes 7½ hours at different temperatures in the kiln. Decals are used on their ceramic Satsuma-like buttons which are hand-decorated with 950 pure liquid gold. Shirley, now 88, occasionally makes buttons, while Stella keeps busy filling her own orders.

Jasperware buttons by Shirley Shaw.

From left: $8.00, $10.00, $8.00.

Mike Edmondson started out making beads, realistic buttons, and marbles, and is now making miniature desk weights. I especially enjoy Mike's glass realistics of which he has quite a variety. He started making his own realistics in 1994, but was not dating his buttons until 1995. In 1996 he started making paperweight buttons, and Mike admits he is still learning and refining his work. He has made very few paperweights in the last two years; he is spending his time experimenting with new glass techniques. His future plans are to make more complex cane setups, including millefiori and making separate canes for his signatures and date. Mike wants to limit the quantity of each design of his realistic buttons and have a number cane on the back. He is self-taught, and button collector Beverly Holgate is credited with encouraging Mike's pursuit in making buttons.

His signature history is as follows:

1995	– E cane
1996	- E6, E96 and ME96 canes
1997	- ME97 cane
1998	- ME98 cane
1999	- ME99 cane
2000	- ME Y2K and ME2000 canes

Skull: Orange base, large clear cap, $20.00.
Butterfly: Millefiori base, butterfly cane in center, $30.00.
Fish: Millefiori base, fish cane in center, $30.00.
Spider: White base, clear cap, $20.00.

Skull, $15.00.

Bottle, $15.00.

Frying eggs, $15.00.

Turtle, $20.00.

Frog, $20.00.

Pumpkin, $15.00.

Fish, $20.00

Pear, $15.00.

Witch, $25.00.

Nancy DuBois makes these darling little purses in her spare time. It allows her to have a little fun and use lots of imagination. The majority of her other buttons require a lot of concentration and attention to detail — one little slip of the hand can ruin the whole button, so these fanciful buttons provide much-needed relief. Using odd leathers, materials, and humorous components, she often achieves a miniature version of a purse you might have owned. Very rarely do two turn out the same, and you'll often find a tiny surprise inside.

Nancy DuBois creations.

Wonderful pink leather purse with beaded handle and dangles on one side. Clasp is a metal hand with beaded cuff closing over a piece of carved and painted pearl. Inside the purse came a tiny little hand-carved comb, metal quarter, and a carved pearl brush with toothbrush bristles. This is my favorite purse button. $35.00.
Beaded Indian purse, leather bottom, tiny feathers, and roped leather drawstring.
Inside is a tiny folded $50.00 bill. $18.00.
Rich-looking tooled leather purse with metal hook closure. $18.00.

More purses by Nancy DuBois.

Scottie dog, fabric and leather with
beaded closure. $12.00.
Engraved polyester with metal
closure and chain handle, $20.00.
Alligator skin with glass eyes, metal
trim, and chain handle, $30.00.

Children, fabric and leather with
beaded closure, $12.00.
Engraved polyester, painted back,
and elastic thread handle, $22.00.
Faux leopard with pearl and plastic
closure and fabric handle, $20.00.

Nancy DuBois has created studio buttons in many different mediums, using a wide range of techniques. Carved, sculpted leather was the first material she used to show her talents. Having acquired leather-working skills as a youth, it seemed natural to try and miniaturize her creations into buttons. As an adult, she started collecting buttons, and with encouragement from a fellow collector, she began taking orders. She made her first buttons in 1992, and since then her variety of subjects and materials has grown considerably. Nancy is self-taught and has given credit to God for her abilities and inspiration. She involves her children as much as possible in the learning process and has often been aided by their ideas and willingness to help with research. DuBois Studio is located on a southern New Jersey farm, surrounded by inspiring landscape and wildlife. In the future, she hopes to learn more in metal working, enameling, and finer glass techniques. Nancy continues to amaze me with her talents and creativity. Many of her pieces are one of a kind.

Pieces by Nancy DuBois.

Lady's Accessories Set in carved and sculpted leather. Each piece of hand-cut and tooled leather has added details, such as ribbons, beads, gold thread, paint, and double-layered cut flowers. This is a very limited set, available briefly in 1996. As with most of her buttons, very few of the same design were made. $90.00 – 100.00 set.

Buttons made by Nancy DuBois.

Ship: Hand-carved and painted leather with twisted leather strips, $35.00.
Grapes: Hand-cut and layered, $10.00.
Mardi Gras mask: Hand-cut, carved, with added details like feathers, paint, and stones, $20.00.

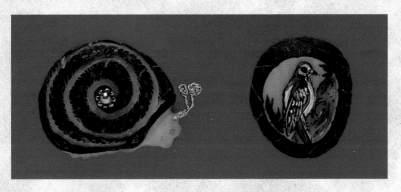

Buttons made by Nancy DuBois.

Snail: Hand-carved vegetable ivory with sterling antenna and embellishment, $35.00.
Woodpecker: Hand painted on a slice of vegetable ivory, $18.00.

Raspberries, reverse painting
on watch crystal, 24k gold foil
and iridescent shell chips sealed
with black resin, $30.00.

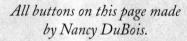

*All buttons on this page made
by Nancy DuBois.*

Platform shoe with goldfish,
reverse-carved and painted
polyester with elastic thread laces,
$22.00.

Rhea bird on manufactured
button, stone set in horn. Nancy
hand-engraved and colored the
bird. $35.00.

Angel and dove, carved and painted wood base with hand-engraved
and painted leather center. $45.00.

Megan Noel has been beading since 1990, and discovered her true calling, bead embroidery, in 1994. She took a class in bead-embroidered buttons from Robin Atkins in the summer of 1997 and has made over 200 since then.

Megan also creates beaded purses, dolls, brooches, and necklaces. But she really enjoys making buttons between her larger projects. They are relatively quick and allow her to express a whimsey not shown in her other work. Megan has developed a fascination with tiny charms to use in her creations. The beading is done over fabric wrapped over a metal frame. She cannot look at anything round without wondering if it could be depicted on a button.

Megan grew up on a sheep farm on Vashon Island and has spent her life around textiles. She now resides in the Artist Republic of Fremont, a neighborhood in Seattle, Washington, and works for Dale Chihuly, world-renowned glass artist.

Frog garden, $40.00.

Christine of C. Resch Studio started making ceramic buttons, then ventured into Plexiglass, which is very time consuming because of the hand cutting and sanding. She has always wanted to work in glass and is now making glass realistics. Most of Christine's buttons are back marked.

Plexiglass Indian Chief, etched and decorated with gold paint, $15.00.

Jim Silva was wearing his leather apron and carving away when Clare and Bob Hatten spotted him at a craft show. Clare was immediately fascinated by his Santa figures. Kathy, his wife, paints all of his carvings. Noticing his magnets with assorted wood heads, Clare asked him if he could make buttons. A few months later, we had 77 international children's head buttons. They were the favor buttons at our dinner for the 1998 Michigan Fall Show. Jim continues to carve, but at this time has no plans to do any more buttons.

$10.00.

These Peruvian buttons are very special, not only because of their craftsmanship, but also for the reason that they were made. Joyce McGrath, a former member of the Michigan Button Society, had a chance encounter with a woman missionary who was selling keychains made by the villagers of Iquitos, Peru, in the Amazon basin. Joyce was immediately impressed and asked the woman if they could make buttons. The next time the missonary came back to the states, she surprised our club with a box load of buttons.

The villagers coat their hands with petroleum jelly before shaping a small ball of resin. A type of tweezers, called pinza, is used to do the detail on the buttons. Some of the buttons are hand molded completely from the resin, while others the resin is molded onto a large fish scale from the piachi fish. The entire button must be molded and detailed within a 10 – 20 minute period or the resin will harden to an unworkable state. The buttons are dried naturally for a minimum of two to four hours. At least two coats of a cinnamon-colored stain are applied to maintain the button's durability. Some of the buttons have Indian seed beads for eyes, but the Shimaco Indian has real piranha fish teeth.

There were 50 buttons of each of the 13 designs. The buttons are signed "Iquitos, Peru." All the money that our club raised was donated to the street children of Peru.

Not shown: Fishing duck, wild duck, iguana, small and large parrot, small and large toucan, dolphin, and toucan on piachi scale.

Boro Indian, $30.00+.
Toucan on piachi scale, $30.00+.

Shimaco Indian, $35.00+.
Jibaro Indian, $30.00+.

Chai Anprasert had been hand carving keychains and animal figures for about 15 years when he met Michigan button collector Ethel Wilson at a craft show in 1997. She tried to convince him that he should try buttons. Since he was still working as an economic specialist for the state of Michigan and had never heard of button collectors, he made no attempts. The following year, Ethel found Chai at the same craft show and struck up a lasting friendship. Since retirement, Chai has been carving and selling his teakwood and walnut buttons at Michigan button shows. He has carved approximately 150 buttons since December 1998. All are signed and dated on the back and have carved wood shanks.

Clockwise from left: Elephant, Kate Greenaway child, Hear No Evil,
turtle, and swan, $7.00 – 10.00 each.

Originally from Conneticut, **Connie Robinson** moved to New York after getting married and opened a ceramic shop in the 1960s. In 1980 she moved to Oregon where she had a store and taught ceramics and porcelain doll making for 13 years. In 1993 she sold the shop and opened a porcelain doll shop in her home.

She started collecting buttons about five years ago and several button collectors asked her to make buttons, and so began her new adventure. Connie now makes over 200 different buttons, all her creations. Her porcelain buttons are painted and highlighted with 22k gold, silver, platinum, or coralene (tiny glass beads fired-on with an adhesive). All her work is signed and dated.

Porcelain buttons by Connie Robinson.

Clockwise from top: Porcelain with rose transfer, covered with coralene and edged in 22k gold, $20.00. 2001 baby doll, painted porcelain with separate moveable arms, $30.00. Little boy's face, painted porcelain (a gift from Connie when my youngest son was born), $25.00. Kewpie doll, painted porcelain, covered in coralene, $30.00.

Kay Ferguson has been developing her skills as an artist for over 20 years. She not only designs and makes buttons but also teaches art to children, and painting and drawing adult education classes at Salem Community College, and owns a stained glass business. She has a bachelor's degree in art and French from Willamette University and obtained master's in education with endorsements in art and French.

In 1994, her high school friend, Jocelyn Howells, saw some of her fused glasswork and asked her if she could make buttons. So began her adventure in the fascinating world of buttons. Kay first draws out the design, then hand cuts the glass from sheets, using a glasscutter and pliers. She assembles the pieces and tacks them together with a small amount of glue. The glue is just to hold the pieces together as she transfers them to the kiln for firing. Kay uses a variety of subjects, including animals, buildings, and insects. Upon special request, she will even do a button of a person's face. All her buttons are signed, dated, and copyrighted.

Her list of button materials is growing. She also uses a laser on myrtle wood, shell, and vegetable ivory buttons. First she draws out the design, then it is scanned into a computer that drives the laser. After she removes the button from the machine, she signs and dates it. Kay is continually captivated and inspired by the beauty and craftsmanship found in old buttons. She has yet to reach her limit of what she would like to create in buttons.

Clown, fused glass, $30.00.

Speaks To Bison, myrtle wood, laser engraved, $10.00.

Shoe with bow, dichroic fused glass, $36.00.

Cat and fishbowl, gray pearl, laser engraved, $12.00.

Cheryl Wood Empson is the daughter of the late James Wilbur Wood, an exceptional carver of Lucite. Mr. Wood made his living by carving clocks, brooches, pendants, penholders, and thermometers from the 1940s through the 1970s. He did all of the carving, sawing, and dyeing. Cheryl, her mother, brother, and sisters all helped with the beveling, sanding, gluing, and other refining tasks. When Mr. Wood went on the road, he sold his items to bars, gifts shops, motels, and grocery stores. Wholesalers made visits to his studio, and he also shipped items to Chicago. Jewelry companies purchased his items and added their own findings.

Cheryl started learning carving in 1990 with her father's encouragement. She carved a few pieces of jewelry in  1998. Her interest in sewing brought her to an online auction site and inevitably to the buttons area. Noticing that there were studio buttons being made by other artists, she decided to try her hand at it. She started carving and selling buttons in 2000, not only for herself but also as a way to honor her father. Collectors have really taken to her work, which is made from leftover Lucite from her father's studio. To date she has made 140 buttons.

Cheryl Wood Empson

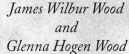

*James Wilbur Wood
and
Glenna Hogen Wood*

*Sunflowers and daisies,
$15.00 – 25.00 each.*

Buttons by Cheryl Wood Empson.

Dolphin, frog, parrot, and fish, $15.00 – 25.00 each.

Diana McClure is very skilled in the pottery arts. After graduating from college with a BFA in ceramics, she set up her studio in Cincinnati. She became a member of several craft guilds and exhibited and sold her hand crafted bowls, pitchers, and assorted functional items at juried art fairs and galleries. Diana made her first clay buttons in 1989.

In 1996 she joined with **Stuart Nedelman** to form the Mud, Metal & Fire, MM&F, Studio. He is a jewelry designer and sells his work to department stores and through craft fairs. Stuart is responsible for the metal work and uses silver castings from his original carvings or ones modified from older designs. He does the soldering and polishing of the metal pieces. Stuart also cuts, shapes, and polishes ivory, antler, bone, and horn, which are used in many of the MM&F buttons. The ivory comes from registered ivory sold legally. The fossilized walrus and mastodon are mined in Alaska. Button collectors seem drawn to the abalone and dyed agate buttons, which have spectacular colored backgrounds. Diana, the button collector of the pair and the partner responsible for much of the design work, matches the metal findings with just the right base material. She then tints the brass and sterling silver castings with enamel paints.

Millennium angel, sterling silver on ivory. Only 12 of these were made, and each button had either a different shape or faceting. The banner around the globe reads "Millennium 2000 and Beyond." There is a similar sterling angel plate on the back, and the ivory is marked with Stuart's signature and the date. Stuart Nedelman. $125.00 – 150.00.

Chimpanzee - Stoneware, original drawn image was pressed into the stoneware. Diana. $6.00.
Porcelain polar bear - The button was created from a plaster press mold made from her original design that was hand carved in clay, then hand painted. Diana. $20.00.
Sailboat - Hand painted porcelain with an applied painted brass ship. MM&F. $28.00.
Eagle - Beautifully detailed cast silver eagle with glass eye, on a natural polished three-dimensional piece of antler, which gives the illusion of the side of a mountain. MM&F. $75.00.

Buttons by Mud, Metal & Fire.
Cat, hand tinted brass cat on abalone shell. MM&F. $24.00.
Lighthouse, hand tinted brass lighthouse on dyed agate. There is ground below, blue green ocean, and white light beaming from the lighthouse. MM&F. $35.00.
Bird, hand tinted brass on picture stone. This is a good example of how Diana picks out just the right material and the way she places the stamping. A bird in flight with sand below, sky above, and hills in the background. MM&F. $26.00.

Herman Lowenstein started making enamel buttons in the late 1970s. The initials HL are etched into the copper back of the poodle button, 1⁹/₁₆", $15.00 – 18.00.

Diane Shewfelt has been making buttons since 1997. She started out making wood buttons, some were woodburned while others were handpainted. In 1998 she collaborated with John Gooderham making paperweight buttons; Diane painted the scenes and John encased them in glass. The buttons were first signed with a J cane and an etched D, later the paperweights had both a J cane and a D cane. Both the paperweight buttons and her wood buttons have themes such as cabins, sailing ships, covered bridges, animals, flowers, and Disney characters.

Diane Shewfelt, woodburned buttons. The lighthouse is signed D Shewfelt 97. The owl is signed D. Lighthouse, $12.00; owl, $8.00.

Christine Shreve's fascination with buttons came when she received her grandmother's collection. Wanting to know more about the buttons, she joined a local button club. In 1999 she decided to try making buttons. She is especially fond of buttons with hand painted figures under glass. Christine calls her buttons "shadowbox buttons" and to date has made 100 buttons. Each button starts out with her hand painting in watercolors on paper. Then the picture and a piece of mineral glass are laminated between two hand cut and sanded frames. All of Christine's buttons have wood shanks, are signed and dated.

Female garden spider, $20.00.

HGW, copper back.
Large, $15.00 – 20.00.

Shirley B, steel back.
Large, $7.00.

Harry G. Wessel made watch crystal buttons with copper backs from 1952 – 1981, using actual glass watch crystals for the tops until the early 1980s. Shortly before his death in 1981, he began to make the tops out of a liquid resin. In 1989 Harry's daughter, **Sara Wolfe,** and his granddaughter, **Shirley Burgess,** decided to continue making the buttons. At the start, this mother-and-daughter team used the same copper back but quickly turned to using steel backs. The steel back is usually painted and has an attached U-shank. The tops are still liquid resin and occasionally will have a painted design on top.

Even though this is a shared effort, you will see only the signature of Shirley B on these watch crystal types. The women are now doing decoupage on plastic and aluminum buttons, and Shirley's son Mike is making hammered and tooled brass buttons, signed Mr. B.

Shirley B, copper back.
Large, $8.00 – 10.00.

Kate McDermid *started making buttons in the early 1990s. She uses fabric from old ties and stretches it over purchased metal forms. On this button, Kate has added a new twist, using the same metal forms with the design done in glass beads. Large, signed K. McD., 98, $12.00.*

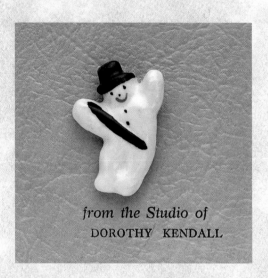

from the Studio of
DOROTHY KENDALL

Kriss Kringle

from the Studio of
DOROTHY KENDALL

Dorothy Kendall *was a ceramic teacher for more than 30 years. Here are three of her holiday buttons on their original cards, but she used all kinds of subjects. The snowman is not dated, but it has her signature mark of a small letter "k" incorporated inside a capital "D." The Santa is signed and dated 1955, while the stocking is signed and dated 1956. Kendall died in 1961. $5.00 – 10.00 each.*

from the Studio of
DOROTHY KENDALL

Melissa Leitch *studied life drawing, print making, and painting at Aquinas College in Michigan. She also has attended workshops at Arrowmount School of Art in Tennessee. She has worked with clay for over 20 years, making hand-built and wheel-thrown pottery. In 1992, she started working with polymer clay, which is man-made plastic clay. To make her face buttons, she fit pieces of clay together in parallel rows so that the cross-section of the "cane" is a face. Thin slices of the cane were pressed onto a disk of raw clay and then fired. Melissa has shown her work at various museums, galleries, and art festivals in Michigan and has won several awards. Of the five faces, only four were given out as the luncheon favor, the fifth face was on a card, which could be purchased to complete the set. There were 30 complete sets made and 50 of the single buttons. Singles, $5.00 – 7.00. Complete set, $35.00 – 40.00.*

Ben Lang *started making buttons of liquid resin in the mid-1960s for his wife, and soon he was selling to other button collectors. Ben used different materials inside of his buttons, such as metal findings, fabric, painted designs, paper cut-outs, and real life objects. He used a cemented-on white metal key shank. All the buttons are signed BenL and are dated between the mid and late 1960s, but I believe he did make a few in the early 1970s.*

I can't remember a time when I wasn't involved in some form of artwork. To me, drawing and painting are just natural pursuits that stem from the sheer wonder of creating images from a world that evolves from within.

In 1972 my introduction to button collecting was the finding of a charm string along with a cache of stunningly beautiful buttons, and a wonderful new love was added to my life. I became immediately absorbed and fascinated with the button world. I wanted to contribute to it, and combining so many of my interests to create hand-crafted buttons gave me a new outlet for my art.

Some of the buttons that I've designed use oil painting, decoupage, china painting, tie buttons, under glass, cross stitched, embroidered, woven raffia, ribbon, pine needle, and reverse painting.

For the past two and a half decades, scrimshaw has been my passion and favorite button endeavor. I find delight in creating an image on the large variety of antique shell buttons. I love the challenge of combining my ideas appropriately with the buttons' characteristics.

History and art brought me knowledge of the scrimshaw of the old sailing vessels. I admire the style, craftsmanship, and ingenuity of the sailors, and it became my inspiration. Schefferly Scrimshaw is accomplished by hand, in the traditional manner employed by the sailing men of long ago.

Subjects are chosen, researched, sketched, and perfected, with a suitable button selected, inspected, prepared, and drafted. Then engraving begins with faithfulness to my original drawing. Each design is achieved by intense labor done outdoors since the dust that is emitted can be a health hazard. There is commitment that goes with each cutting. No erasures or false moves are allowed. Next comes the pigmenting, sanding, and polishing that eventually reveals the image. Then even more cutting, staining, and polishing. I hold my breath until I can see that no cracks, chips, or crevasses appear to hold pigment in unsuspected places. If the brittle substance of the shell does not break through this process or under the strain of engraving, I complete the button. What was once just blank raw material at the start of the long journey has become transformed into a beautiful object.

I prefer to execute my work with natural materials and have engraved on vegetable ivory, horn, bone, wood, deer and moose antlers, and all manner of shell. Some types of plastic and metals, plus a few other materials have also proved to be quite favorable.

I strive for unique, new, and exciting areas to explore. Thus, my scrimshaw buttons are extremely limited editions, usually with two buttons per image, sometimes only one. To this date I have never executed more than eight buttons of any one drawing, and that was an unusually rare case.

Although my buttons of the late 1970s and early 1980s can have a number of different backmarks, each Schefferly Scrimshaw button is engraved with my signature, date, number, and catalog number.

I love to watch reactions as people view my work. As an artist, it's truly rewarding

— **Diane Schefferly**

Facing page, three buttons in corners from top left:

Butterfly – two-piece, carved rim, $35.00.
Hummingbird – square, green snail shell, $35.00.

Center panel, clockwise from top:

Fish – smoky pearl, $15.00.
Japanese court lady with cat, smoky Tahitian pearl, $90.00.
Frog reading book on lilypad, dark irregular pearl, $65.00.
Alice in Wonderland with White Rabbit – four hole sew-thru, mother-of-pearl, $110.00.
Sailing ship – two hole sew-thru, nautilus shell, $75.00.

Buttons by Diane Schefferly.

I purchased these buttons from dealer/collector Jeanne Talbert in the mid 1990s. She purchased them from creator Emanuel Dethier's daughter. In 1947, Dethier and his family emigrated to Hungary from Germany and made and sold buttons for added income. The buttons are unsigned and were never very popular with button collectors, a sad but true fact for many of the buttons that come from cottage industries. Sizes range from small to large, white and red ceramic, unglazed backs, sew-thrus and self shanks. $3.00 each.

Glass Mounted in Metal

Light pink glass, mounted in an openwork frame with protruding facetted metal, 1¼", $18.00 – 22.00.

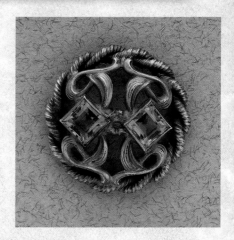

Openwork metal, with two yellow glass stones, 1⁵/₁₆", $25.00.

These circa 1870 – 1910 lacy-type buttons are mounted in metal. The first, second, and fifth buttons are black glass with different lusters. The smaller third and fourth buttons are partial black glass and opaline glass. Buttons range in size from ⁹/₁₆" to 1¼". Small, $6.00. Medium, $10.00 – 15.00. Large, $15.00 – 20.00.

Drum buttons are medium in size, have straight-sided rims, and are at least ³/₁₆" high. Medium, $12.00, $8.00, $18.00.

Large jewel button, back-marked Made in Czecho-slovakia, 1⁹/₁₆", $25.00.

Large jewel button, back-marked Gesetzlich and Geschutzt (legal, trademarked, patent, etc.). 1⁹/₁₆", $25.00.

Gay 90s, large faceted center stone, black lacquered steel back with loop shank. 1³/₄", $35.00.

Gay 90s, oblong center stone, mounted under an ornate brass frame with two cut steels. Black lacquered steel rim, heavy wire shank. 1⁷/₈", $45.00.

Gay 90s, openwork metal, oval stone surrounded by eight claw-set pastes. 1³/₄", $75.00.

Gay 90s, openwork metal, faceted center stone surrounded by three cut steels. 1³/₄", $60.00.

Faceted blue glass, mounted in brass with cut steel embellishments. 1½", $35.00 – 45.00.

Oval cabochon mounted in stamped and painted brass. 1³⁄₁₆" x 1⅝". $20.00.

Pierced paste button with champlevé enamel around the edges. Medium, 1¹⁄₁₆", $35.00 – 45.00.

Dome-shaped faceted black glass center set in brass with black glass embellishment. 1½", $30.00.

The first three are design under glass, described as one-piece brass mounting, with no separate rim, and glass covering the design. The last button has the same one-piece mounting but has a heavy loop shank and is considered a small jewel button. Three of the four buttons have channel-set stones around the border. Left to right: Medium, $18.00. Small, $8.00. Small, $8.00. Small, $10.00.

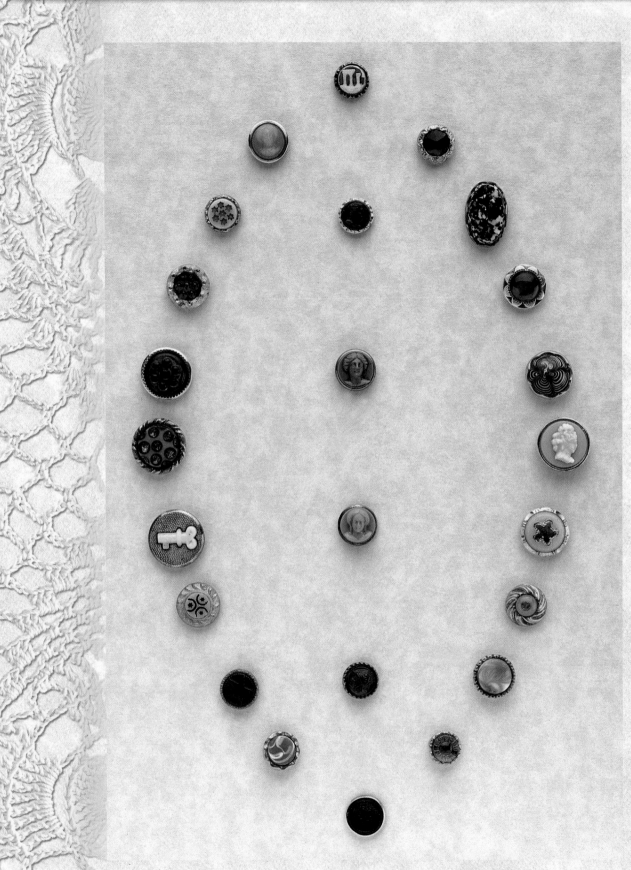

An assortment of small jewel buttons. $7.00 – 18.00 each.

*Prong-set pastes surrounding a
large cabochon set in silver with
a copper shank. 1⅜", $55.00.*

*Molded green glass mounted in a
white metal frame.
1¼" x ⅞", $12.00 – 16.00.*

*Superior quality paste and glass stone buttons.
¹¹⁄₁₆" to 1⅛", $12.00 – 20.00 each.*

Assorted Materials

This is an example of one of my work in progress cards of six-pointed stars.

Row 1: Vegetable ivory, small, $6.00. Horn, back-marked Breveté, S.G.D.G., medium, $10.00. Openwork metal with cut steel embellishment, large, $18.00.
Row 2: Drum, pearl chips under reverse painted glass, medium, $12.00. Clambroth glass with black transfer design, medium, $18.00.
Row 3: One-piece brass, stamped and engraved, large, $20.00. White molded glass, top painted black, small, $12.00. Pearl, sew-thru, medium, $8.00.

Cinnabar set in metal, back-marked
Silver and China, $^{13}/_{16}$", $35.00.

Wood, from $^7/_8$" to $1^3/_4$".
Dog, $12.00. Skier, $10.00. Horse and foal, $5.00. Painted boat scene, $5.00.

Horatio Seymour & Franci P. Blair, Jr. were the
presidential and vice-presidential Democratic candidates
in 1868. Seymour lost to the widely known Civil War
general, Ulysses S. Grant. This rubber button is considered
rare and is back-marked N.R. Co., Goodyear's P=T. 1851.
$350.00 – 450.00.

The majority of examples shown here are from the mid to late 1800s. Horn buttons were made from the hooves and horns of cows, goats, and buffalo. The horn had to be soaked and boiled for many weeks, then split open and laid flat between heated iron plates. The horn sheets were scraped clean with a knife and then polished. Up to 12 buttons could be made in a heated mold that contained the patterned dies. The buttons were left natural or dyed, with black being the prevalent color. Horn buttons in general have a slight roughness or grain on the back. Some have a small hole on the back called a "pick mark," left when the buttons were lifted from the mold. The smell of burning hair is present when tested with a hot needle. Buttons pictured range in size from ⅞" to 1¹³⁄₁₆". Top center: Green man's face in the middle of foliage, $18.00. Top right: Natural, with eight cut steels, $12.00. Middle left: Odin, $25.00. Middle center: Rooster head, $50.00. Bottom center: Natural, with molded moons and pearl inserts, $25.00. Miscellaneous heads, $10.00 – 18.00.

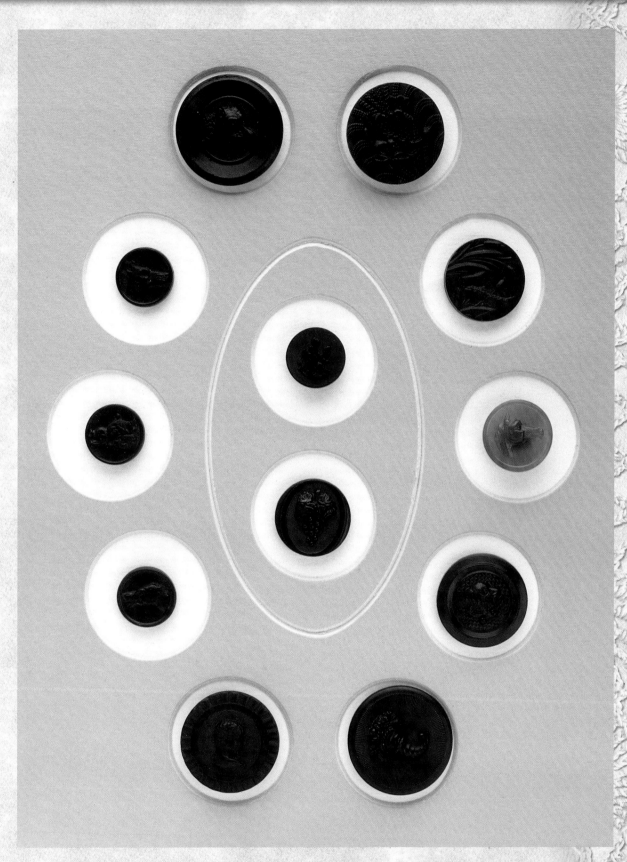

More horn buttons, ranging in size from small to medium. Clockwise: Rose and insect, $6.00;
fish, $8.00; horse head, $8.00; dog with whip, $8.00; cornucopia, $10.00; Mercury, $10.00;
dog head, $7.00; boar head, $7.00; wolf head, $7.00; wolf head, $9.00.
Center: Girl with lamb, $10.00; bunch of grapes, $12.00.

Vegetable ivory buttons are made from the corozo or tagua nut of a palm. The outside of the nut is dark brown with a cream-colored center. It can be cut, carved, dyed, and painted, and manipulated by numerous other techniques also.

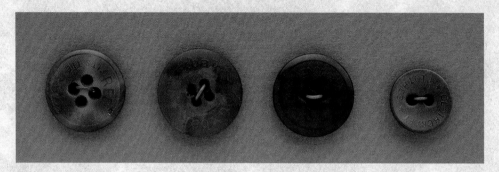

Left to right: Clothcraft clothes, $2.00; dry back or money back, $6.00; duxback, $4.00; Red Head Fits the Sport, $6.00.

Left to right: Glass center, $15.00; painted scene, circa 1940s, $8.00; metal watch wheel and red glass center, $15.00; fabric sew-thru, $4.00; carved and pierced, $8.00.

Left to right: Butterfly, $12.00; modified square with flowers, $5.00; realistic ladybug, $25.00 – 35.00; anchor, $6.00; swastika, $10.00; mah jongg tile, $15.00.

More vegetable ivory buttons.

Clockwise: Carved, $6.00; pierced, $8.00; three-hole, $8.00; dyed (red), $3.00; pearl center, $15.00; stenciled, $8.00; baseball, $20.00; crocheted center, $8.00; leaf, $8.00; metal star escutcheon, $15.00.
Center row: Lily of the valley, $5.00; grapes, $8.00; Cupid chasing butterfly, $20.00; horseshoe and whip, $8.00.

Huge gutta-percha chrysanthemum on wood, held in place by two screws on the back, loop shank. 1⅞", $50.00.

Pressed wood center, picturing the fable "Fox and the Crane." Brass rim, steel back, and wire shank. 1⅝", $50.00.

Stamped brass on wood, held in place by two rivets. Large, $18.00.

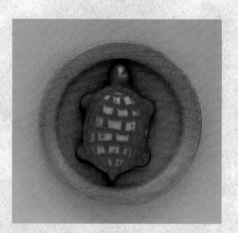

Celluloid turtle on wood. Large, $18.00.

Wood with red Bakelite. From left, $10.00; $8.00; $6.00.

Molded wood composition (Syrocco or Burwood), large, except for crest button.

Scotty head, $15.00. Leaf, $7.00. Acorn (realistic), $12.00. Elephant, $20.00. Floral shape, $8.00. Soldier on horse, $25.00. House and carriage, $35.00. Barrel (realistic), $10.00. Sailboat, $12.00. Crest, $8.00.

Molded composition wood button,
nice shape. Large, $30.00.

This lithograph button has always been
called Count Axel von Fersen. Reference
has also been made to a younger depiction
of Louis XVI. Decorative border.
1¼", $38.00.

Vest buttons with center materials like gemstones, pearl, enamel, and pottery. $10.00 – 20.00.

*Carved ivory. Left: Small, $20.00.
Right: Medium, $35.00.*

*Moss agate mounted in brass with a
separate gold rim. Medium, $25.00.*

Composition, small and medium, $5.00 – 12.00 each.

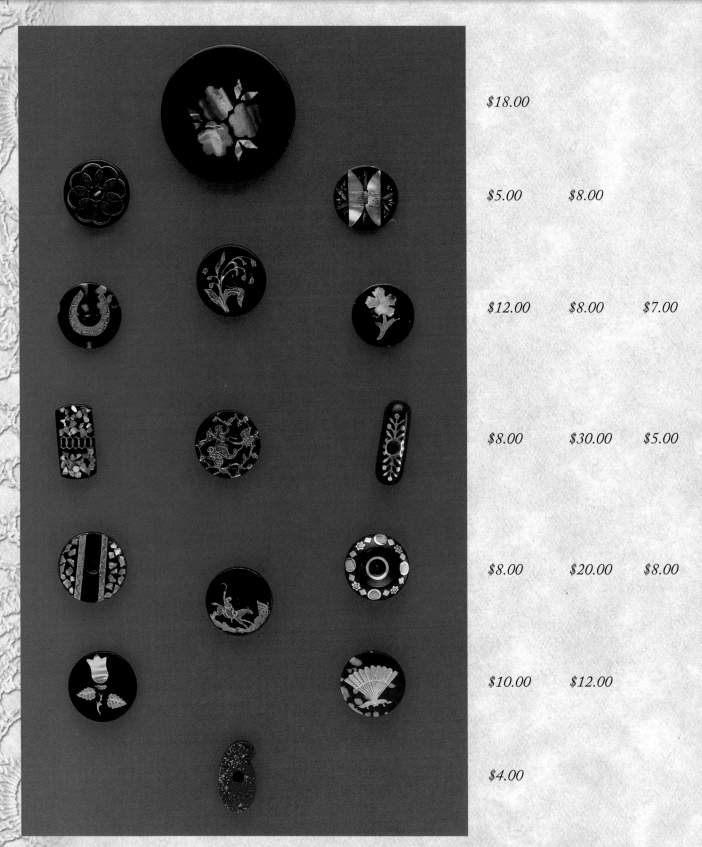

$18.00

$5.00 $8.00

$12.00 $8.00 $7.00

$8.00 $30.00 $5.00

$8.00 $20.00 $8.00

$10.00 $12.00

$4.00

These inlay buttons, $^{11}/_{16}$" to $1^7/_{16}$", are made of composition, papier-maché and /or horn. The added white metal, brass, pearl chips, and pearl cut-out pieces can be quite pleasing to the eye. On some, the decoration was pressed into the surface of the button while still warm. On the large papier-maché button, the floral cut-outs were glued on top and covered with several coats of varnish. I especially enjoy finding pictorial metal inlays to add to my collection.

Porcelain Studs

From top, left to right:

$30.00; $15.00; $30.00.
$24.00; $22.00.
$20.00; $18.00.
$30.00; $18.00; $22.00.

237

Diminutives

To be classed as a diminutive, a button must measure ⅜" or smaller and pass through either the Lindley or NBS diminutive measurement hole. Working on a tray of 72 diminutives can be both challenging and pleasureable.

Facing page, from top:

Row 1: Mounted in metal
Waist coat, glass overlay and goldstone, $5.00. Mirror mounted in metal, $2.50.

Row 2: Bone
Tinted bone buttons, $4.00 each.

Row 3: China
Calico, $6.00; birdcage shank, $3.00; birdcage shank, $2.00; three-hole, $3.00.

Row 4: Enamels
Pierced, $6.00; fly, realistic, $12.00; square, $7.00; shaped, $5.00.

Row 5: Assorted
Painted wood, $3.00; velvet background, $3.00; woven thread center, $5.00; floral on horn, $6.00.

Row 6: Glass moonglows
Lime, $8.00; light blue, $3.00; candy striped, $5.00; candy striped, $5.00; oval, $3.00.

Row 7: Glass
Cobalt, $6.00; Gooderham paperweight, $15.00; peacock eye, $18.00; lavender Victorian, $5.00; two-piece Czech, $3.00.

Row 8: Studio buttons by Nancy DuBois
Engraved floral design on pen shell, embellished with rhinestones. $15.00. Engraved pen shell of a hot-air balloon, gold paint-filled lines, embellished with rhinestones, $20.00. Glass purse paperweight with silver foil coins and a rhinestone for a snap closure, $22.00.

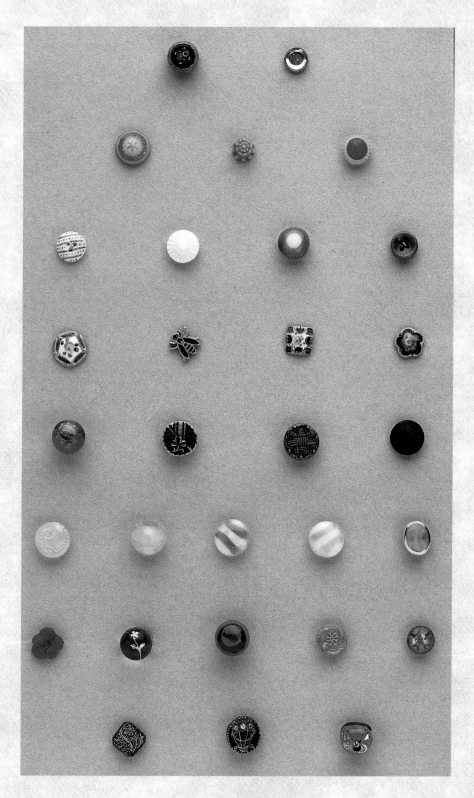

Diminutives in assorted materials.

Buckles

Egyptian woman's head applied to a decorative stamped brass background, 5" x 2¼", $50.00.
Stamped brass, Huntsman and his Kill, applied to a circular openwork brass clasp, 3" x 1¼", $35.00.
Stamped brass clasp with applied cut steels, in the shape of a fan. This buckle is identical to the
button that collectors call Madame Chrysanthéme, 3½" x 1⅝", $45.00.

Heavy brass buckle with brass leaves and three green glass stones, 1920s, 3½" x 1⅝", $30.00.
Openwork metal surrounding blue glass cabochons, mounted on an odd-shaped white metal
base, 1930s, 4¼" x 1³⁄₁₆", $35.00.
This clasp has a steel rim surrounding a decorative brass center with 38 glass stones and black
lacquered steel back, 1910, 3½" x 1⅞", $45.00.

Top: *This fabulous snake clasp has the word Sterling and the number 366 on the back as well as the hallmark of the William B. Kerr Co. of Newark, New Jersey, founded in 1855 and purchased by Gorham in 1906.*
4¾" x 1¾", $400.00.
Bottom: *Black Bakelite clasp with a metal escutcheon of a Gibson Girl head, 6¾" x 1¾", $60.00.*

Heavily gilt filigree brass with prong-set stones.
Marked Made in Czechoslovakia on hook, 1920s.
2¹¹⁄₁₆", $30.00.

This floral enamel clasp has snakes intertwined on multicolored green foliage. Stamped into the metal back are the words Metal and Gilt. 2¹³/₁₆" x 1½", $100.00 – 125.00.

Opaque and transparent green enamel clasp, 3" x 2", $70.00 – 85.00.

This glass cane buckle is marked Czechoslovakia on the back of the metal hook, 1⅝", $25.00.

Celluloid clasp, 1920s, $30.00.
Two coconut shell buckles, 1950s, $10.00 – 15.00 each.

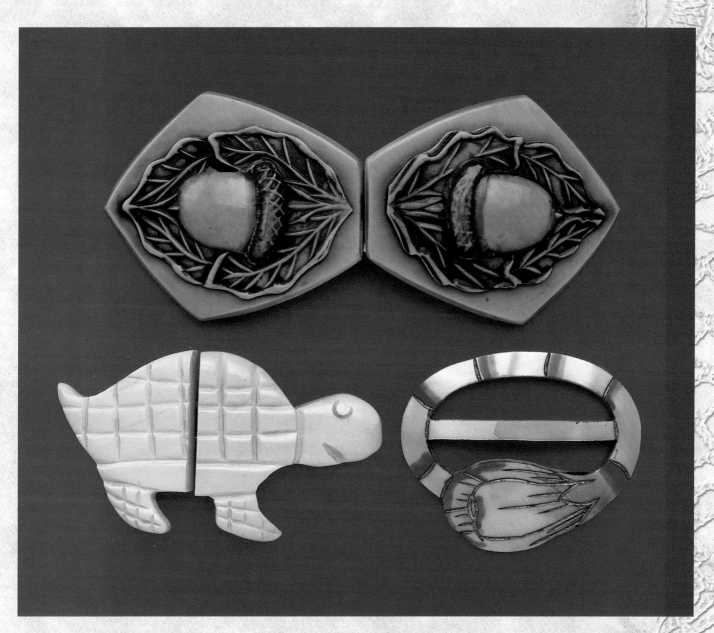

Celluloid clasp, 4⅝" x 2". $35.00 – 45.00.
Bakelite turtle clasp, 3⅞" x 1¼". $125.00.
Celluloid buckle. $18.00.

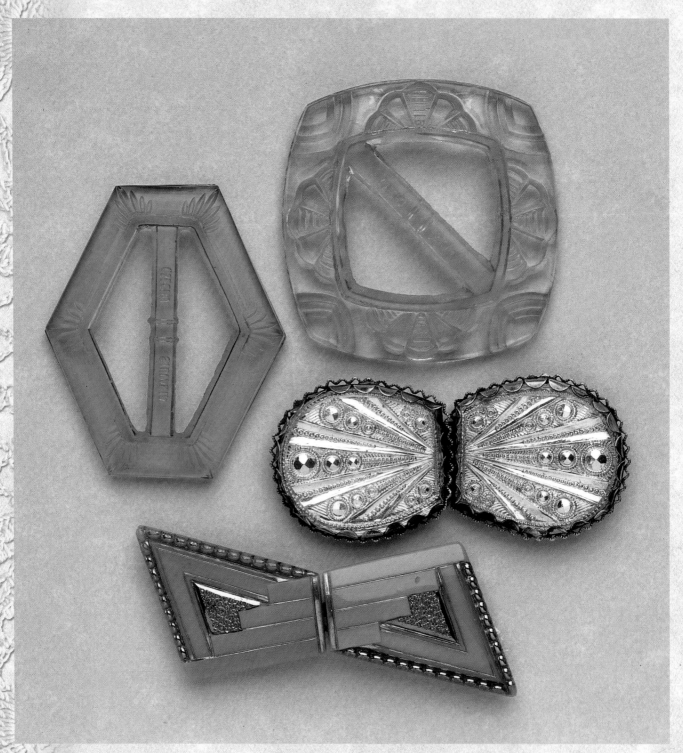

Assorted glass buckles.

Clockwise from top left: Green and pink buckles marked Czecho-Slovakia, $10.00 each.
Foil backed glass set in metal, back marked Made In Czecho-slovakia. 2¹¹/₁₆", $35.00.
Tan two-piece buckle with gold and silver luster, 2½", $20.00.

Shoe Buckles

This pair of shoe buckles has hundreds of individually riveted cut steels with black satin underneath, back-marked France. 2¹⁄₁₆", $40.00 pair.

Metal beads and cut steels on a fabric-covered frame. The clip part on the back is marked Holfast Pat App For and France, 1860s. $65.00 pair.

Individual riveted cut steels in a butterfly pattern, back-marked France. 2³⁄₁₆", $50.00 pair.

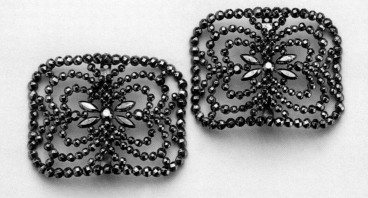

Shirt Studs

Pair of faceted black glass studs. $20.00.

Hand painted porcelain ladies' cuff links. $35.00

Bridle Rosettes

Horse bridle rosettes. $30.00 – 40.00 each.

Bibliography

Albert, Lillian Smith and Kathryn Kent. *The Complete Button Book,* CT, John Edwards, 1971.

Brown, Dorothy Foster. *Button Parade.* Chicago, IL: Lightner Publishing, Reprint 1968.

Chamberlin, Erwina and Minerva Miner. *A Button Heritage.* Sherburne, NY: Heritage Press, 1967.

Clark, Ruth Miller. *A Carnival of Iridescent Luster Buttons.* 1986.

———. *A Carnival of Iridescent Luster Buttons – Book II.* 1992.

Couse, L. Erwina and Marguerite Maple. *Button Classics.* Chicago, IL: Lightner Publishing, 1941.

Epstein, Diana and Millicent Safro. *Buttons.* New York, N.Y., Henry N. Abrams, 1991.

Fields, Pat and David. *From Nut to Button.* 2001.

Fink, Nancy and Maryalice Ditzler. *Buttons.* Philadelphia, PA: Courage Books, 1993.

Hughes, Elizabeth and Marion Lester. *The Big Book of Buttons.* Sedgwick, ME: New Leaf Publishers, Reprint, 1991.

Jargstorf, Sibylle. *Baubles, Buttons and Beads.* Angler, PA: Schiffer Publishing, 1993.

Leslie, Hane S. *A Reference Book on Studio Button Makers.* 1997.

Luscomb, Sally C. *The Collector's Encyclopedia of Buttons.* Atglen, PA: Schiffer Publishing, Reprint, 1992.

McGrath, Gerald H. and Janet Meana. *Fashion Buckles — Common to Classic.* Atglen, PA: Schiffer Publishing, 1997.

Osborne, Peggy Ann. *About Buttons — A Collectors' Guide.* Atglen, PA: Schiffer Publishing, 1994.

———. *Button, Button Identification & Price Guide.* Atglen, PA: Schiffer Publishing, 1993.

———. *Fun Buttons.* Atglen, PA: Schiffer Publishing, 1994.

Perry, Alan G. *A Carnival of Iridescent Luster Buttons – Book III.* 1995.

Smith, Lillian Albert and Jane Ford Adams. *The Button Sampler.* New York, NY: Gramercy Publishing Company, 1951.

Wisniewski, Debra J. *Antique and Collectible Buttons.* Paducah, KY: Collector Books, 1997.

Zacharie, Florence and Ellis Nicholls. *Button Handbook.* Sedgwick, ME: New Leaf Publishers, Reprint, 1994.

Periodicals:

Just Buttons Magazine, 1943 – 1979.

National Button Society Bulletins, 1942 to present.

Resources

Button Bug – Debra J. Wisniewski
dbuttons@iserv.net
www.iserv.net/~dbuttons
I sell vintage buttons, mounting wire, cleaning pads, and of course, my button books.
Buttonlovers chat group: http://groups.yahoo.com/group/buttonlovers/

Button Cottage
P.O. Box 15
Fontana, WI 53125
www/thebuttoncottage.com
Limited edition Battersea buttons.

C&B Weiser
7189 Brantford Road
Dayton, OH 45414-2352
Phone: 937-890-9987
www.cbweiser.com
Connie and Bud have a large inventory of modern, vintage, and studio buttons they sell at various
button shows. Bud makes a wide assortment of deluxe mounting boards and is always willing to
take special requests. Button measures, display frames, and out of print button books can also be
purchased.

Cheryl Wood Empson
ladylucite@hotmail.com
e-Bay ID: ladylucite
www.ladylucite.com
Cheryl makes reverse carved and dyed buttons from her father's vintage Lucite stock.

Connie Robinson
580 Portland Ave
Roseburg, OR 97470
541-672-0850
shalimar@mcsi.net
www.geocities.com/dragonbutton/ConnieR/shalimar.html
High quality porcelain buttons

Diane Schefferly
3903 W. Cedar Lk. Rd.
Greenbush, MI 48738
Phone: 989-739-3956
dses@i-star.com
Large variety of hand done scrimshaw buttons, designed on mother-of-pearl, celluloid, horn, and
bone. Each button is signed, dated, and numbered by Diane.

E.S. DuBois III
Phone: 856-935-9686
dimi1@mindspring.com
Skip's paperweight buttons are a delight to own. His florals are the most realistic available to collectors today, and the craftmanship of his paperweights is unrivaled.

John Gooderham
57 Raymond St.
Sault Ste. Marie, Ontario
Canada P6C 2E5
John is a well-known, long-time maker of paperweight buttons.

Nancy DuBois
Phone 856-935-9686
dimi1@mindspring.com
Dealer for Nancy's buttons is Ann Frazier of Pennsylvania, 215-862-9560.
Nancy's talents enable her to make buttons from leather, engraved shell, paperweights, carved vegetable ivory, wood, and more.

National Button Society
Lois Pool, secretary
2733 Juno Place
Akron, OH 44333-4137
Annual membership: $20.00 adults, due by December 1, each year; after December 1, $25.00
Lifetime: $300.00. Juniors (8 – 15 years old), $2.00 annually

O'Gosh Buttons
2411 Doty St.
Oshkosh, WI 54902
www.ohgosh-buttons.com
Kathy carries a large inventory of new Czech Republic moonglows and a variety of vintage buttons. She also has past issues of *Just Buttons* magazines and National Button Society bulletins.

Index

Index

COLLECTOR BOOKS
Informing Today's Collector

DOLLS, FIGURES & TEDDY BEARS

2079	**Barbie** Doll Fashion, Volume I, Eames	$24.95
3957	**Barbie** Exclusives, Rana	$18.95
6022	The **Barbie** Doll Years, 5th Edition, Olds	$19.95
3810	**Chatty Cathy** Dolls, Lewis	$15.95
4559	Collectible **Action Figures**, 2nd Ed., Manos	$17.95
2211	Collector's Ency. of **Madame Alexander Dolls**, 1965 – 1990, Smith	$24.95
4863	Collector's Encyclopedia of **Vogue Dolls**, Stover/Izen	$29.95
5904	Collector's Guide to **Celebrity Dolls**, Spurgeon	$24.95
1799	**Effanbee Dolls**, Smith	$19.95
5611	**Madame Alexander** Store Exclusives & Limited Editions, Crowsey	$24.95
5689	**Nippon Dolls** & Playthings, Van Patten/Lau	$29.95
5253	Story of **Barbie**, 2nd Ed., Westenhouser	$24.95
1513	**Teddy Bears & Steiff** Animals, Mandel	$9.95
1808	Wonder of **Barbie**, Manos	$9.95
1430	World of **Barbie** Dolls, Manos	$9.95
4880	World of **Raggedy Ann** Collectibles, Avery	$24.95

TOYS & MARBLES

2333	Antique & Collectible **Marbles**, 3rd Ed., Grist	$9.95
2338	Collector's Encyclopedia of **Disneyana**, Longest, Stern	$24.95
5681	Collector's Guide to **Lunchboxes**, White	$19.95
4566	Collector's Guide to **Tootsietoys**, 2nd Ed, Richter	$19.95
5360	**Fisher-Price Toys**, Cassity	$19.95
4945	**G-Men and FBI Toys**, Whitworth	$18.95
5593	Grist's Big Book of **Marbles**, 2nd Ed.	$24.95
3970	Grist's Machine-Made & Contemporary **Marbles**, 2nd Ed.	$9.95
5267	**Matchbox Toys**, 3rd Ed., 1947 to 1998, Johnson	$19.95
5830	**McDonald's** Collectibles, Henriques/DuVall	$24.95
5673	Modern **Candy Containers** & Novelties, Brush/Miller	$19.95
1540	Modern **Toys** 1930–1980, Baker	$19.95
5920	Schroeder's Collectible **Toys**, Antique to Modern Price Guide, 8th Ed	$17.95
5908	**Toy Car** Collector's Guide, Johnson	$19.95

JEWELRY, HATPINS, & PURSES

1748	Antique **Purses**, Revised Second Ed., Holiner	$19.95
4850	Collectible **Costume Jewelry**, Simonds	$24.95
5675	Collectible **Silver Jewelry**, Rezazadeh	$24.95
3722	Collector's Ency. of **Compacts**, Carryalls & Face Powder Boxes, Mueller	$24.95
4940	**Costume Jewelry**, A Practical Handbook & Value Guide, Rezazadeh	$24.95
5812	Fifty Years of Collectible Fashion **Jewelry**, 1925-1975, Baker	$24.95
1424	**Hatpins** & Hatpin Holders, Baker	$9.95
5695	**Ladies' Vintage Accessories**, Bruton	$24.95
1181	100 Years of Collectible **Jewelry**, 1850 – 1950, Baker	$9.95
6039	Signed Beauties of **Costume Jewelry**, Brown	$24.95
4850	Unsigned Beauties of **Costume Jewelry**, Brown	$24.95
5696	Vintage & Vogue Ladies' **Compacts**, 2nd Edition, Gerson	$29.95
5923	**Vintage Jewelry** for Investment & Casual Wear, Edeen	$24.95

FURNITURE

3716	American **Oak** Furniture, Book II, McNerney	$12.95
1118	Antique **Oak** Furniture, Hill	$7.95
2132	Collector's Encyclopedia of **American** Furniture, Vol. I, Swedberg	$24.95
3720	Collector's Encyclopedia of **American** Furniture, Vol. III, Swedberg	$24.95
5359	Early **American** Furniture, Obbard	$12.95
1755	Furniture of the **Depression Era**, Swedberg	$19.95
3906	**Heywood-Wakefield** Modern Furniture, Rouland	$18.95
1885	**Victorian** Furniture, Our American Heritage, McNerney	$9.95
3829	**Victorian** Furniture, Our American Heritage, Book II, McNerney	$9.95

INDIANS, GUNS, KNIVES, TOOLS, PRIMITIVES

1868	Antique **Tools**, Our American Heritage, McNerney	$9.95
1426	**Arrowheads** & Projectile Points, Hothem	$7.95
5616	Big Book of **Pocket Knives**, Stewart	$19.95
2279	**Indian Artifacts** of the Midwest, Hothem	$14.95
5685	**Indian Artifacts** of the Midwest, Book IV, Hothem	$19.95
5826	**Indian Axes** & Related Stone Artifacts, 2nd Edition, Hothem	$19.95
6132	Modern **Guns**, Identification & Values, 14th Ed., Quertermous	$14.95
2164	**Primitives**, Our American Heritage, McNerney	$9.95
1759	**Primitives**, Our American Heritage, Series II, McNerney	$14.95
6031	Standard **Knife** Collector's Guide, 4th Ed., Ritchie & Stewart	$14.95

PAPER COLLECTIBLES & BOOKS

4633	**Big Little Books**, A Collector's Reference & Value Guide, Jacobs	$18.95
5902	**Boys' & Girls' Book** Series, Jones	$19.95
4710	Collector's Guide to **Children's Books**, 1850 to 1950, Jones	$18.95
5596	Collector's Guide to **Children's Books**, 1950 to 1975, Jones	$19.95
1441	Collector's Guide to **Post Cards**, Wood	$9.95
2081	Guide to Collecting **Cookbooks**, Allen	$14.95
2080	Price Guide to **Cookbooks** & Recipe Leaflets, Dickinson	$9.95
3973	**Sheet Music** Reference & Price Guide, 2nd Ed., Pafik & Guiheen	$19.95
4733	**Whitman Juvenile Books**, Brown	$17.95

OTHER COLLECTIBLES

5898	Antique & Contemporary **Advertising Memorabilia**, Summers	$24.95
5814	Antique **Brass & Copper** Collectibles, Gaston	$24.95
1880	Antique **Iron**, McNerney	$9.95
3872	Antique **Tins**, Dodge	$24.95
5607	Antiquing and Collecting on the **Internet**, Parry	$12.95
1128	**Bottle** Pricing Guide, 3rd Ed., Cleveland	$7.95
3718	Collectible **Aluminum**, Grist	$16.95
4560	Collectible **Cats**, An Identification & Value Guide, Book II, Fyke	$19.95
5676	Collectible **Souvenir Spoons**, Book II, Bednersh	$29.95
5666	Collector's Encyclopedia of **Granite Ware**, Book II, Greguire	$29.95
4857	Collector's Guide to **Art Deco**, 2nd Ed., Gaston	$17.95
5906	Collector's Guide to **Creek Chub Lures** & Collectibles, 2nd Ed., Smith	$29.95
3966	Collector's Guide to **Inkwells**, Identification & Values, Badders	$18.95
3881	Collector's Guide to **Novelty Radios**, Bunis/Breed	$18.95
4652	Collector's Guide to **Transistor Radios**, 2nd Ed., Bunis	$16.95
4864	Collector's Guide to **Wallace Nutting Pictures**, Ivankovich	$18.95
5929	Commercial **Fish Decoys**, Baron	$29.95
1629	**Doorstops**, Identification & Values, Bertoia	$9.95
5683	**Fishing Lure Collectibles**, 2nd Ed., Murphy/Edmisten	$29.95
5911	**Flea Market Trader**, 13th Ed., Huxford	$9.95
5262	**Fountain Pens**, Erano	$24.95
3819	**General Store** Collectibles, Wilson	$24.95
2216	**Kitchen Antiques**, 1790–1940, McNerney	$14.95
5686	**Lighting Fixtures** of the Depression Era, Book I, Thomas	$24.95
4950	The **Lone Ranger**, Collector's Reference & Value Guide, Felbinger	$18.95
5603	19th Century **Fishing Lures**, Carter	$29.95
5835	**Racing Collectibles**	$19.95
2026	**Railroad** Collectibles, 4th Ed., Baker	$14.95
5619	**Roy Rogers and Dale Evans** Toys & Memorabilia, Coyle	$24.95
1632	**Salt & Pepper Shakers**, Guarnaccia	$9.95
5091	**Salt & Pepper Shakers** II, Guarnaccia	$18.95
3443	**Salt & Pepper Shakers** IV, Guarnaccia	$18.95
5007	**Silverplated Flatware**, Revised 4th Edition, Hagan	$18.95
6040	**Star Wars** Super Collector's Wish Book, Carlton	$29.95
3892	**Toy & Miniature Sewing Machines**, Thomas	$18.95
3977	Value Guide to **Gas Station Memorabilia**, Summers	$24.95
4877	Vintage **Bar Ware**, Visakay	$24.95
5925	The Vintage Era of **Golf Club** Collectibles, John	$29.95
4935	The W.F. Cody **Buffalo Bill** Collector's Guide with Values, Wojtowicz	$24.95

GLASSWARE & POTTERY

4929	**American Art Pottery**, 1880 – 1950, Sigafoose	$24.95
5907	Collector's Encyclopedia of **Depression Glass**, 15th Ed., Florence	$19.95
5748	Collector's Encyclopedia of **Fiesta**, 9th Ed., Huxford	$24.95
5609	Collector's Encyclopedia of **Limoges Porcelain**, 3rd Ed., Gaston	$29.95
1358	Collector's Encyclopedia of **McCoy Pottery**, Huxford	$19.95
5677	Collector's Encyclopedia of **Niloak**, 2nd Edition, Gifford	$29.95
5678	Collector's Encyclopedia of **Nippon Porcelain**, 6th Series, Van Patten	$29.95
5618	Collector's Encyclopedia of **Rosemeade Pottery**, Dommel	$24.95
5842	Collector's Encyclopedia of **Roseville Pottery**, Vol. 2, Huxford/Nickel	$24.95
5921	Collector's Encyclopedia of **Stangl Artware**, Lamps, and Birds, Runge	$29.95
5680	Collector's Guide to **Feather Edge Ware**, McAllister	$19.95
2339	Collector's Guide to **Shawnee Pottery**, Vanderbilt	$19.95
1523	Colors in **Cambridge Glass**, National Cambridge Society	$19.95
4714	**Czechoslovakian Glass** and Collectibles, Book II, Barta	$16.95
5528	Early American **Pattern Glass**, Metz	$17.95
5257	**Fenton Art Glass** Patterns, 1939 – 1980, Whitmyer	$29.95
5261	**Fostoria Tableware**, 1924 – 1943, Long/Seate	$24.95
5899	**Glass & Ceramic Baskets**, White	$19.95
5840	**Heisey Glass**, 1896 – 1957, Bredehoft	$24.95
5691	**Post86 Fiesta**, Identification & Value Guide, Racheter	$19.95
6037	**Rookwood Pottery**, Nicholson/Thomas	$24.95
5924	**Zanesville Stoneware** Company, Rans, Ralston & Russell	$24.95

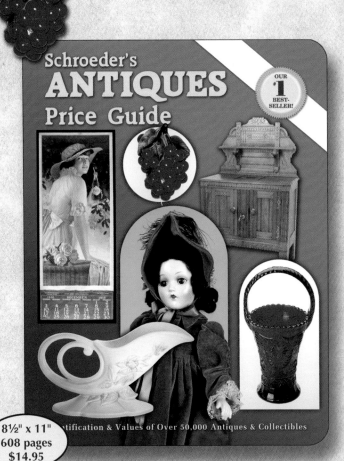